C000171695

CONTENT

 @lfc   liverpoolfc   liverpoolfc

Reach Sport

Editor David Cottrell **Assistant Editor** William Hughes **Writer** Chris McLoughlin **Production Editor** Michael McGuinness **Design** Colin Sumpter
Photography Press Association, Getty Images, Liverpool Echo, John Powell, Andrew Powell, Nicholas Taylor © Liverpool Football Club & Athletic Grounds Ltd.
Published by Reach Sport
Managing Director Steve Hanrahan **Commercial Director** Will Beedles **Executive Art Editor** Rick Cooke **Executive Editor** Paul Dove
Marketing & Communications Manager Claire Brown **Website** www.reachsportshop.com **Printed by** William Gibbons

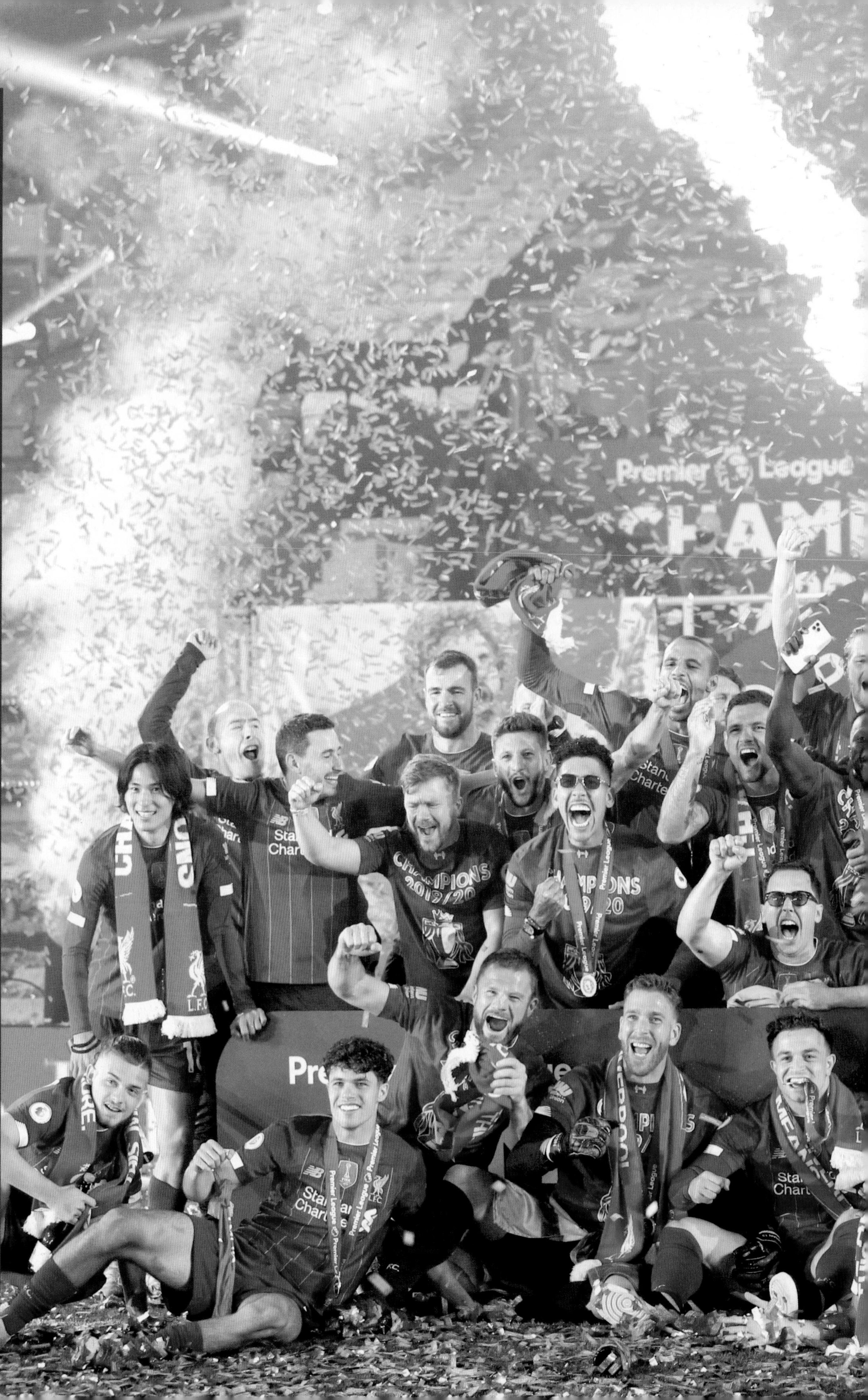
Premier League
CHAMPIONS 2019/20

CHAMPIONS 2019/20

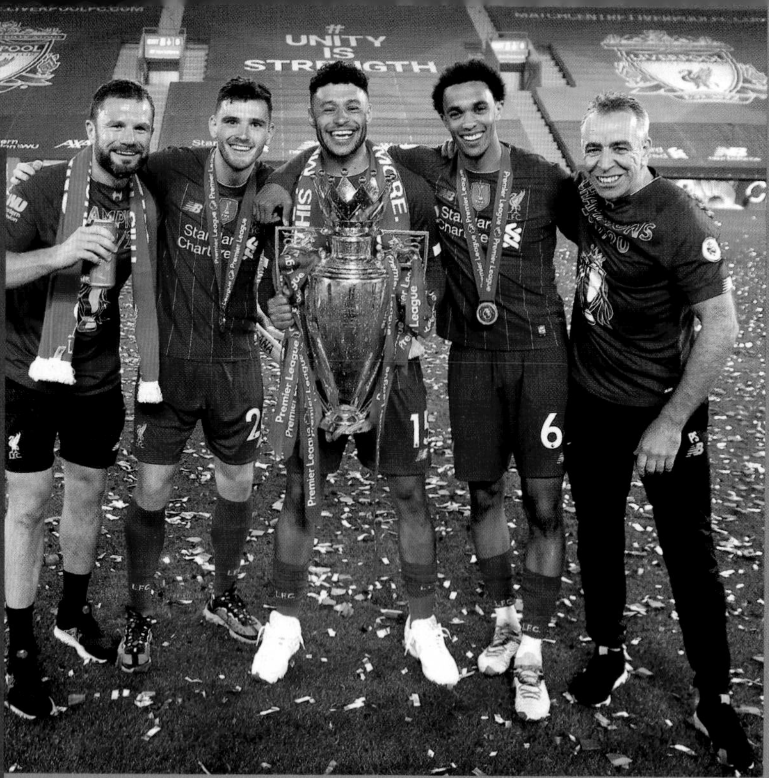

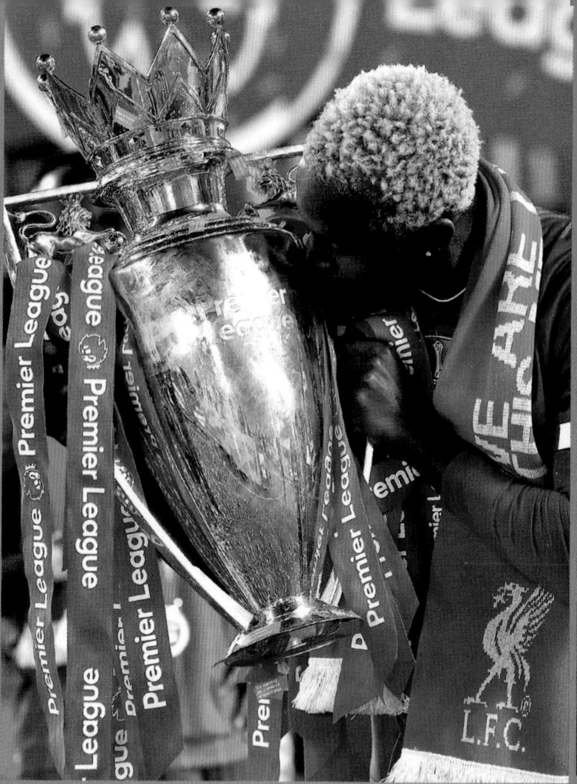

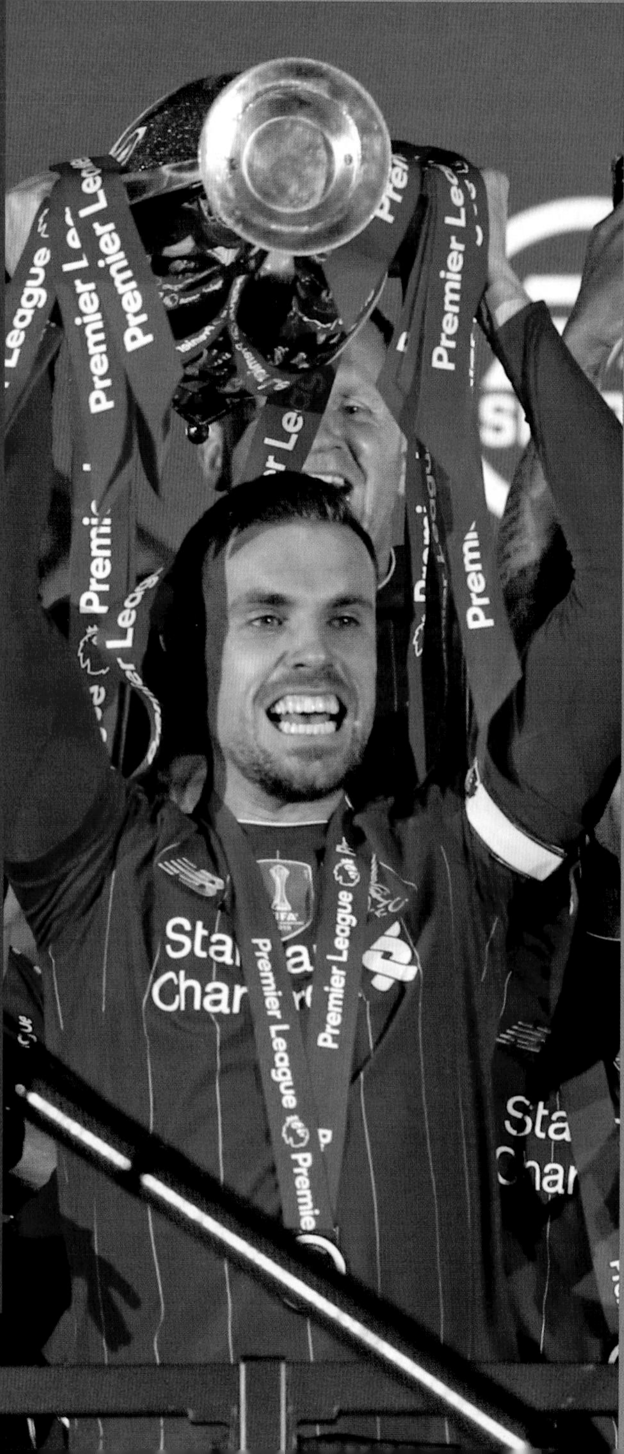

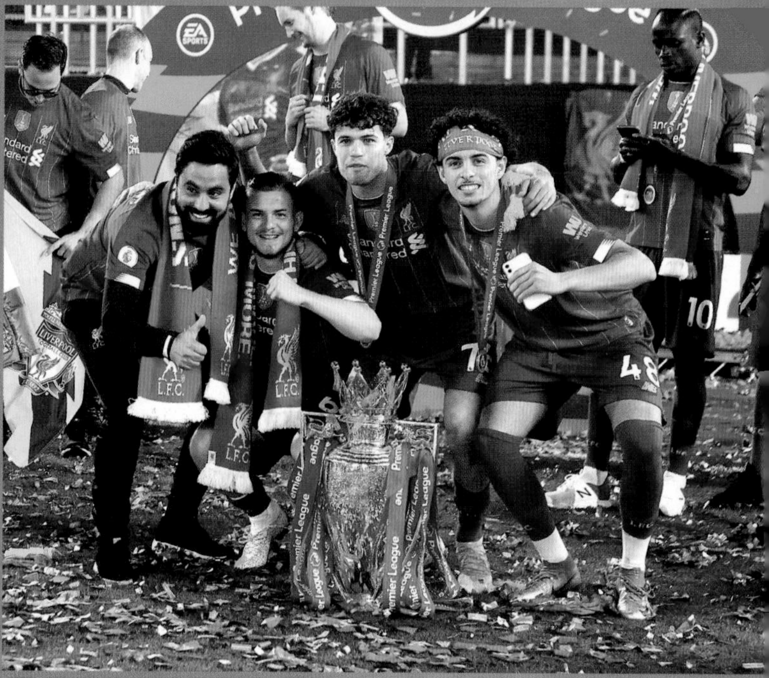

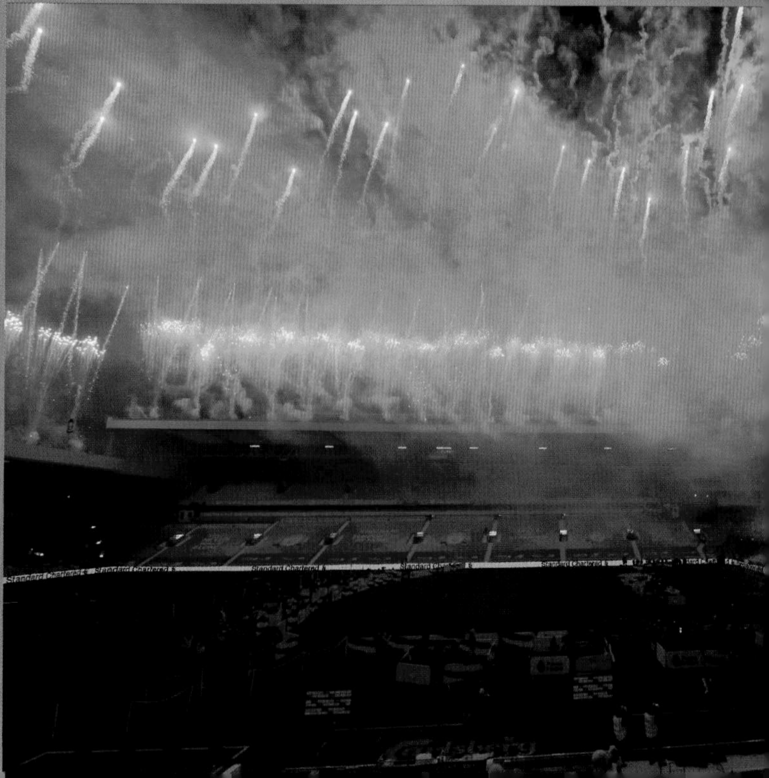

CHAMPIONS 2019/20

CHAMPIONS 2019/20

LIVERPOOL 4
NORWICH CITY 1

Goals: Hanley (7og), Salah (19), van Dijk (28), Origi (42); Pukki (64)

09.08.19 • Anfield • Attendance: 53,333
Referee: Michael Oliver

LIVERPOOL (4-3-3): Alisson (Adrian 39), Alexander-Arnold, Gomez, van Dijk, Robertson, Fabinho, Henderson (C), Wijnaldum, Salah, Firmino (Milner 86), Origi (Mane 74).
Subs not used: Keita, Oxlade-Chamberlain, Shaqiri, Matip.

NORWICH CITY (4-2-3-1): Krul, Aarons, Hanley (C), Godfrey, Lewis, McLean, Trybull (Hernandez 70), Buendia, Stiepermann, (Leitner 58), Cantwell, Pukki (Drmic 83).
Subs not used: Fahrmann, Byram, Roberts, Vrancic.
Booked: Leitner, Buendia.

PRESS BOX:

ANDY DUNN, THE MIRROR

"An exquisite finish from one of your world class strikers? Tick. A thumping header from your Ballon d'Or-standard colossus? Tick. A joyous romp to celebrate the start of another season under possibly the most charismatic manager in club football? Tick."

PUNDIT:

GIANFRANCO ZOLA, BEIN SPORTS

"It was a comfortable win. They started very well, very strong and showed the quality that they have. Liverpool is a team that, every game, concedes something to the opposition, but if they get away and not concede then when they have chances themselves their conversion rate is unbelievable."

LIVERPOOL v NORWICH CITY

MANAGER: JÜRGEN KLOPP

"For 60 minutes we looked very sharp, then we have to control the game a bit more. Norwich have all my respect – they stayed cheeky, they enjoyed their football. At the start of the second half we could have scored a fifth or sixth goal, then Norwich scored. After that we were never in danger but had to work hard to keep the score what it was."

FOR THE RECORD:

Liverpool extended their run of scoring at least four goals in one league game every season since 1920/21, the longest run in English football.

ALSO THIS WEEKEND:
- West Ham United 0-5 Manchester City
- Manchester United 4-0 Chelsea
- Tottenham Hotspur 3-1 Aston Villa

REPORT:

Friday night and I like the way you move, Divock Origi. On his 100th appearance for Liverpool the Belgian striker picked up where he left off in Madrid in June with a goal and an assist as the Reds got their 2019/20 Premier League campaign off to a flying start with four first-half goals at Anfield.

Origi's header, Liverpool's fourth, was his 29th for LFC and made him the 13th player in the club's history to have scored on every day of the week. Jamie Webster's Whigfield-inspired tribute song for Origi could now have a verse for all seven days.

Long before he nodded home from a pinpoint Trent Alexander-Arnold cross – the fifth consecutive PL game the right-back has assisted in – Origi had created Liverpool's seventh minute opener himself, firing in a low cross that Norwich skipper Grant Hanley slashed into his own net from the edge of the six yard box.

It wasn't the first time a Norwich player had scored the Reds' first league goal of a season – Steve Bruce did the same against Joe Fagan's European champions in 1984 – but this was the first time LFC have ever netted four first-half goals in their opening league match.

They did so, however, against a lively Canaries side who have got a couple of exciting, attacking midfielders in the shape of Emi Buendia and Todd Cantwell. They, along with striker Teemu Pukki, gave the impression that Daniel Farke's side will score goals at this level, but they also looked likely to concede them.

Mo Salah and Roberto Firmino, the two best players on the pitch, combined sublimely for Liverpool's second with the Egyptian King taking Firmino's return pass and slotting past Tim Krul. And it was from a Salah corner that Virgil van Dijk headed home the Reds' third, before there was a shock at the other end of the pitch. Alisson injured his calf taking a goal kick and had to be helped off immediately, an injury that would thrust a summer signing straight into the spotlight.

On came Spanish goalkeeper Adrian, to a rapturous Kop reception, to make his debut and it was soon 4-0 when Origi headed past Krul. The Dutch keeper also denied Firmino before the interval and pushed Jordan Henderson's shot onto the bar after it, keeping a clean sheet as the Reds attacked the Kop end following half-time.

Norwich made a game of it in the second half – Moritz Leitner hit the crossbar and forward Pukki pulled a goal back – but the game was long over by then, even if the season was just getting started.

SOUTHAMPTON 1
LIVERPOOL 2

Goals: Ings (83); Mane (45), Firmino (71)
17.08.19 • St Mary's • Attendance: 31,712
Referee: Andre Marriner

SOUTHAMPTON (3-5-2): Gunn, Bednarek, Yoshida, Vestergaard, Valery, Ward-Prowse, Romeu (Ings 64), Højberg (C), Bertrand (Djenepo 77), Adams (Armstrong 68), Redmond. Subs not used: Forster, Cedric, Obafemi, Danso. Booked: Romeu, Djenepo.

LIVERPOOL (4-3-3): Adrian, Alexander-Arnold, Matip, van Dijk, Robertson, Oxlade-Chamberlain (Henderson 89), Wijnaldum, Milner (C) (Fabinho 74), Salah (Origi 79), Firmino, Mane. Subs not used: Lonergan, Gomez, Lallana, Shaqiri. Booked: Alexander-Arnold.

PRESS BOX:
PAUL ROWAN, SUNDAY TIMES
"Klopp preferred to emphasise that the 'mentality giants are back in town' and he had a point. Adrian lined up behind a Liverpool team boasting Salah, Firmino and Mane together for the first time since the Champions League final in Madrid. That formidable trio looked in the mood to tear Southampton apart."

PUNDIT:
DANNY MURPHY,
BBC MATCH OF THE DAY
"Mane, in 2019, has scored 20 goals, more goals than anyone else in the Liverpool side, and he is becoming more than just a goalscorer. He's got great pace to run in behind, as we know, which stretches teams and his goal was a moment of magic. People don't think of Mane as being a provider, but his assists are good as well."

MANAGER: JÜRGEN KLOPP
"I like the reaction today a lot; coming here and fighting for three points like they were the last three points ever in the Premier League. That's the attitude which brought us to the finals we played and that's what we have to continue."

FOR THE RECORD:
Jürgen Klopp became the quickest LFC manager to reach 300 points in the three points for a win system, doing so in his 146th game – four fewer than Kenny Dalglish (150), and further clear of Rafa Benitez (159), Bob Paisley (161) and Bill Shankly (166).

ALSO THIS WEEKEND:
• Manchester City 2-2 Tottenham Hotspur
• Norwich City 3-1 Newcastle United
• Aston Villa 1-2 Bournemouth

REPORT:
Less than a month before this Premier League clash at the home of his former club, Sadio Mane was playing for Senegal in the Africa Cup of Nations final against Algeria in Egypt. Along with Crystal Palace's Cheikhou Kouyate and Manchester City's Riyad Mahrez, no other Premier League players had a shorter summer break.

Yet just like on Wednesday night when Liverpool won the UEFA Super Cup against Chelsea on penalties in Istanbul following a 2-2 draw, Mane was involved in both Liverpool goals. He was named as man-of-the-match.

"Fitness, tiredness, is in here," he had said, tapping the side of his head during a press conference before the UEFA Super Cup final. "For a long time now I've never had a break. For seven years I've never had a holiday longer than 20 days."

At St Mary's he looked fresher than a breeze blowing in off the Solent and it was his arrowed 45th minute strike, after receiving a James Milner pass and cutting inside on the edge of the box, that gave the Reds the lead at the end of a tricky first-half.

Liverpool could have easily been behind by then, Adrian producing a fine save from Maya Yoshida and Che Adams heading a good chance over, but they weren't and assumed control following Mane's opener.

Roberto Firmino ended a flowing move by firing just wide and Joel Matip almost diverted a shot by Milner – who had to leave the field for stitches to a head-wound during the first-half and returned wearing a Basil Fawlty-style bandage – into the Saints' goal before the Brazilian made it 2-0 in the 71st minute.

Mane won possession from a Southampton throw-in deep in their half and slipped the ball to Firmino, who cut across the Saints box. Despite there being six home defenders between him and the goal, he somehow still managed to find the net with a precise low drive.

That looked to be that, but when Adrian's attempted clearance flew into the net off Danny Ings it gave Southampton hope and they almost turned that into a 2-2 draw.

Former Liverpool striker Ings, who remains a popular figure amongst Kopites, had a glorious chance to nick a late equaliser only to turn the ball wide from close range with the goal at his mercy.

So Liverpool escaped with all three points, and a club-record equalling 11th consecutive Premier League win, while Mane took his 2019 goals tally for the Reds to 20, eight more than any of his team-mates have managed.

The rest of the division should be thankful he doesn't get a longer summer break.

15

GAME 3

LIVERPOOL v ARSENAL

LIVERPOOL 3
ARSENAL 1

Goals: Matip (41), Salah (49pen, 58); Torreira (85)
24.08.19 • Anfield • Attendance: 53,298
Referee: Anthony Taylor

PRESS BOX:
DAVID MADDOCK, DAILY MIRROR
"Arsenal were never allowed to breathe. They were dispossessed in their own defensive third eight times in the first half. That's the most by any team this season, and the most for Arsenal in a decade. One of the best passing teams in Europe was effectively transformed into a long-ball minnow because of the claustrophobic pressure."

PUNDIT:
JOHN ALDRIDGE, LIVERPOOL ECHO
"In the first half, their closing down and pressing was exactly what Jürgen Klopp will have asked for before the game. Trent Alexander-Arnold and Andy Robertson were flashing inviting deliveries across the six-yard box time and again. For the likes of me, Ian Rush and Robbie Fowler, they were made for us."

LIVERPOOL (4-3-3): Adrian, Alexander-Arnold, Matip, van Dijk, Robertson, Henderson (C), Fabinho, Wijnaldum (Milner 69), Salah, Firmino (Lallana 86), Mane (Oxlade-Chamberlain 77). Subs not used: Kelleher, Gomez, Shaqiri, Origi. Booked: Fabinho.

ARSENAL (4-2-3-1): Leno, Maitland-Niles, Sokratis, Luiz, Monreal, Xhaka (C), Guendouzi (Mkhitaryan 86), Willock (Lacazette 81), Ceballos (Torreira 61), Pepe, Aubameyang. Subs not used: Martinez, Chambers, Nelson, Kolasinac. Booked: Luiz.

REPORT:
A new banner bearing the phrase 'The Unbearables' was held aloft on the Kop before kick-off and on the evidence of this convincing 3-1 victory against Arsenal it won't be long until one with 'The Relentless Reds' appears next to it.

Not only did Jürgen Klopp's side rack up a club record-equalling 12th successive league win, they did so by playing a relentless, intense, incessant style of football that Unai Emery's Gunners simply couldn't deal with.

Implementing a diamond formation, that allowed full-backs Trent Alexander-Arnold and Andy Robertson acres of space on the flanks, was a strange tactical decision by the Arsenal manager. It played into Liverpool's hands, but it was the way the Reds pressed, harried and pressurised their opponents that earned them another three points to maintain a perfect start to the season.

Kicking towards the Kop in the first half, Liverpool hemmed the visitors in for long periods and it almost paid dividends when attacking midfielder Dani Ceballos, who'd dropped incredibly deep into his own half to gain possession, tried a cross-field pass that went straight to Sadio Mane in the penalty area. Only a Bernd Leno save kept out the Senegalese striker's effort on goal.

Shortly before that, at the other end of the pitch, Arsenal had almost scored on the counter-attack through Pierre-Emerick Aubameyang, a player Klopp knows well from their time together at Borussia Dortmund.

Aubameyang's attempted through-ball to Nicolas Pepe was intercepted by Adrian as he rushed out of his penalty area, but he

16

→

LIVERPOOL v ARSENAL

only managed to direct his clearance straight back to Aubameyang. The Gabon international striker controlled the ball and lobbed it goalwards from 20 yards, but it dropped wide of the empty net as Joel Matip raced back towards the goalline.

If Adrian got away with one there he redeemed himself when Pepe ran clean through after the Gunners cleared a Liverpool corner. The Arsenal winger's shot lacked power, but Adrian still had to dive to his right to make a block.

Despite those opportunities on the break, it was no surprise when the Reds took the lead in the 41st minute. Alexander-Arnold swung over a corner and Joel Matip headed home his first Kop-end goal with the Arsenal defence preoccupied by Virgil van Dijk's presence.

Mo Salah was causing Arsenal all sorts of problems and when David Luiz tugged his shirt in the box four minutes after the interval, referee Anthony Taylor pointed to the spot. Salah curled the penalty

into the top corner like he was bending a free-kick around a wall, but there was better to come from the Egyptian.

Fabinho turned a pass into Salah's direction close to the half-way line. As Luiz came across to challenge him, Salah flicked the ball past the Brazilian defender – taking him out of the game completely – and rapidly raced clear of Nacho Monreal before slotting a composed finish into the bottom corner. 3-0. It was Salah at his electric best and Arsenal were a beaten team.

A late consolation strike from Lucas Torreira put the Gunners on the scoresheet, but Liverpool have now hit 26 goals against Arsenal in eight league games under Klopp's management, none of which he has lost. More pertinently, by the time round three of the Premier League fixtures were completed, the Redmen were leading the way as the only team in the division to have a 100% record.

On this form, the relentless Reds must be unbearable to play against and they'll take some shifting from the top of the table.

MANAGER: JÜRGEN KLOPP

"The intention was to be us, just be us. Our identity is intensity, and the intensity we put into the game was really incredible. It was a performance full of power, energy, greed and passion, which I think you need against a team like Arsenal."

FOR THE RECORD:
This was Liverpool's 12th consecutive top-flight victory, equalling the club record set between April and October 1990.

ALSO THIS WEEKEND:
• Aston Villa 2-0 Everton
• Manchester United 1-2 Crystal Palace
• Tottenham Hotspur 0-1 Newcastle United

BURNLEY 0
LIVERPOOL 3

Goals: Wood (33og), Mane (37), Firmino (80)
31.08.19 • Turf Moor • Attendance: 21,762
Referee: Chris Kavanagh

BURNLEY (4-4-2): Pope, Lowton, Tarkowski, Mee (C), Pieters, Lennon, Westwood, Cork, McNeil, Wood, Barnes (Rodriguez 73).
Subs not used: Hart, Taylor, Drinkwater, Hendrick, Vydra, Long.

LIVERPOOL (4-3-3): Adrian, Alexander-Arnold, Matip, van Dijk, Robertson, Henderson (C) (Oxlade-Chamberlain 71), Fabinho, Wijnaldum, Salah, Firmino (Shaqiri 85), Mane (Origi 85).
Subs not used: Kelleher, Milner, Gomez, Lallana.

PRESS BOX:

PAUL GORST, LIVERPOOL ECHO

"The sight of the flamboyant Brazilian dancing his way through the celebrations irked a home crowd who seemingly care little for that kind of fancy. It was a sight to behold for the visitors however as they toasted their return to the top."

PUNDIT:

LOUIS SAHA, STADIUM ASTRO

"For me, Sadio Mane is the most consistent one. He's dangerous in every game. He is underrated in terms of the rankings for the 2018 Ballon d'Or. The Ballon d'Or rankings surprised me – he wasn't even in the top 10. For me, it's a shocker." [Mane then finished 4th in 2019]

BURNLEY v LIVERPOOL

20

W

MANAGER: JÜRGEN KLOPP

"We scored a bit of a lucky goal, but I think we still deserved that we were 1-0 up. The second goal, brilliant. Just brilliant. Winning the ball, really quick decision-making and then a super pass from Bobby and a super finish from Sadio. The third goal, brilliant."

FOR THE RECORD:

Not only was this a club-record 13th consecutive top-flight win, the Reds also became the first side since Spurs in 1960 to score at least twice during all 13 victories.

ALSO THIS WEEKEND:

• Manchester City 4-0 Brighton & Hove Albion
• Arsenal 2-2 Tottenham Hotspur
• Chelsea 2-2 Sheffield United

REPORT:

When the history books look back on the Jürgen Klopp era at Liverpool a couple of decades from now, Roberto Firmino will be talked about in the same way Ray Kennedy is when assessing Bob Paisley's reign as LFC manager.

Kennedy was signed as a striker by Bill Shankly shortly before his Anfield departure in 1974, but converted to a left-sided midfielder by Paisley. He went on to score 72 goals in a red shirt.

Firmino was signed as a wide midfielder by Brendan Rodgers shortly before his Anfield departure in 2015, but has been converted to a centre forward by Klopp. His goal in this 3-0 win at Burnley was his 50th in the Premier League and his 68th for the Reds. Just like Kennedy in the 1970s, the Brazilian is a classic example of how a coach can get the best out of a player – and team – by switching his position. At Turf Moor, Firmino was at his brilliant best.

Yet football is a team game and without an important second minute save by Adrian, who kept his first clean sheet for Liverpool, and a slice of luck for the opening goal, this ultimately cosy win in East Lancashire could've become as uncomfortable as previous visits here have been.

Mo Salah twice came closest to scoring in the opening half hour, hitting the post and seeing the ball rebound off his shins and roll wide after Nick Pope dived at his feet, before the opener came via the boot of Trent Alexander-Arnold. The right-back's attempted cross clipped Burnley striker Chris Wood and looped over Pope into the net.

There's a joke about Pope being beaten from a cross in there somewhere, but Klopp wasn't laughing when told in a post-match TV interview that the Premier League had adjudicated it to be a Wood own goal rather than one for Alexander-Arnold. "You're kidding?" he frowned. "How is that possible?"

Burnley boss Sean Dyche must have been wondering how it was possible for his side to gift the Reds a second goal, but that's precisely what happened four minutes after Liverpool's first when Clarets skipper Ben Mee passed the ball straight to Firmino, who promptly played Sadio Mane in to slot home.

Firmino's moment of history – he became the first Brazilian to score 50 goals in English football's top-flight – followed 10 minutes before the end of the second half. After slipping Joel Matip's clearance into Salah's path, Firmino sprinted forward and the ball fell kindly to him on the edge of the box. He rifled it into the bottom corner.

Game over, records broken and, most importantly, the Reds headed into the September international break top of the Premier League with the only 100% record in all four divisions.

LIVERPOOL 3
NEWCASTLE UNITED 1
Goals: Mane (28, 40), Salah (72); Willems (7)
14.09.19 • Anfield • Attendance: 51,430
Referee: Andre Marriner

LIVERPOOL (4-3-3): Adrian, Alexander-Arnold, Matip, van Dijk (C), Robertson, Oxlade-Chamberlain (Milner 75), Fabinho, Wijnaldum (Shaqiri 84), Salah, Mane, Origi (Firmino 37). Subs not used: Kelleher, Gomez, Henderson, Lallana.

NEWCASTLE UNITED (3-5-2): Dubravka, Krafth (Manquillo 67), Schar (Fernandez 80), Lascelles (C), Dummett, Willems, Almiron (Muto 67), Hayden, Shelvey, Atsu, Joelinton. Subs not used: Darlow, Clark, Ki, M Longstaff.

PRESS BOX:
MATTHEW SYED, THE TIMES
"Liverpool are the first Premier League side to win 14 successive matches while scoring more than one goal in each, a testament to their continuing revolution. They have many fine individual players but, like all the best teams, it is the whole rather than the parts that impress the most. Firmino is the player, perhaps more than any other, that helps to knit the whole together."

PUNDIT:
GRAEME SOUNESS, SKY SPORTS
"They are a team I don't think anyone enjoys playing against because they are aggressive and they test every part of your game with the physicality and technique they all have. It's unusual in the modern game, but they have players who are willing to point fingers at team-mates if they are not at it. That makes them very, very strong."

MANAGER: JÜRGEN KLOPP
"In the moment when we were more flexible on Sadio and Bobby's position and when we used Mo more often for balls into his feet and one-twos in and around the box, we were then really in charge of the game. We won a lot of second balls and there were not so many counter-attacks anymore, so it was then a really good game."

FOR THE RECORD:
Liverpool have now scored 101 Premier League goals against Newcastle United, the first opponents the Reds have reached a century against in the Premier League era, extending a PL record of scoring in 24 home matches in a row against the same opposition.

ALSO THIS WEEKEND:
• Norwich City 3-2 Manchester City
• Wolverhampton Wanderers 2-5 Chelsea
• Bournemouth 3-1 Everton

REPORT:
On a sunny Saturday afternoon when Roberto Firmino produced one of the most outrageous assists Anfield has seen, it was Sadio Mane who set a Premier League record.

Mane's first half double took his tally to 19 goals in his last 21 home appearances and extended his record of having never lost a game at Anfield in which he has scored to 35 – 33 wins and a couple of draws. Yet an even more impressive statistic emerged.

Liverpool's 3-1 victory was Mane's 50th Premier League game for the Reds at Anfield. He's lost none of them, making him the first player in Premier League history to go half-a-century of games unbeaten at one stadium for the same club.

Add in his sole Anfield appearance for Southampton, a 1-1 draw, and his overall tally is 51, but it says a lot about the Reds' remarkable home form that Mo Salah is second on the list.

This was the Egyptian's 41st Premier League game for Liverpool without losing at Anfield and, like Mane, he was also on the scoresheet, but it took the arrival of Roberto

Firmino to spark the Redmen into life.

Newcastle took the lead in the seventh minute through a powerful drive by left wing-back Jetro Willems. They led for 21 minutes, the longest the Reds had been behind for at home in 30 games, although quite how they avoided conceding a penalty when Joel Matip was dragged to the floor by Jamaal Lascelles was baffling given the presence of VAR.

Mane's 28th minute equaliser, a soaring, angled-strike from Andy Robertson's pass, had Newcastle reeling and when Firmino came on for Divock Origi, who twisted his ankle, nine minutes later they simply couldn't contain Liverpool's front three.

Firmino wins the ball like Ian Rush did but also can also pass it like Kenny Dalglish. He'd only been on the pitch for three minutes when he did both, robbing Christian Atsu and sending Mane clean through. Magpies keeper Martin Dubravka got to the ball first, but only pushed it against Mane, who gladly tapped it over the line.

Liverpool's third goal was a thing of beauty. Salah passed the ball into Firmino who, with

his back to goal, dragged the ball behind him with his right foot before back-heeling it sideways into Salah's path with his left. By the time Newcastle realised what had happened the ball was in their net. Game over.

Trent Alexander-Arnold, twice, and Robertson could both have added to Liverpool's tally, but 3-1 was enough to put the Reds five points clear at the top as Anfield purred thanks to the best front three in the business.

CHELSEA 1
LIVERPOOL 2

Goals: Kante (71); Alexander-Arnold (14), Firmino (30)

22.09.19 • Stamford Bridge • Attendance: 40,638
Referee: Michael Oliver

CHELSEA (4-3-3): Arrizabalaga, Azpilicueta (C), Christensen (Zouma 40), Tomori, Emerson (Alonso 15), Kante, Jorginho, Kovacic, Willian, Abraham (Batshuayi 77), Mount.
Subs not used: Caballero, Barkley, Pedro, Pulisic.
Booked: Tomori, Kovacic, Alonso.

LIVERPOOL (4-3-3): Adrian, Alexander-Arnold, Matip, van Dijk, Robertson, Henderson (C) (Lallana 84), Fabinho, Wijnaldum, Salah (Gomez 90), Firmino, Mane (Milner 71).
Subs not used: Kelleher, Oxlade-Chamberlain, Shaqiri, Brewster.
Booked: Alexander-Arnold, Fabinho, Milner.

PRESS BOX:
JOHN CROSS, DAILY MIRROR
"Trent Alexander-Arnold and Joel Matip were outstanding in defence, Fabinho superb in midfield. And the lung-busting run by left-back Andy Robertson in injury time to ease mounting Chelsea pressure typified Liverpool's spirit."

PUNDIT:
ROY KEANE, SKY SPORTS
"There are times to be self-critical but if you told them before the game you'd win 2-1, they'd have took it. If they win the league they won't look back at this result thinking 'we could have done better there' – they'll just be happy to have the medal in their hands."

REPORT:

Liverpool are on a roll and it was making the ball roll that paved the way for this club-record seventh straight away league win at Chelsea. Both of the Reds' goals came from set-pieces involving Trent Alexander-Arnold, but only after they got the ball moving.

Stamford Bridge has long been a difficult place for Liverpool to visit – between 1990 and October 2008 the Reds won just once in 24 visits to Chelsea – so it was always going to be a tough test in Jürgen Klopp's 150th Premier League game in charge.

But, when you're on a club-record run of 14 consecutive league wins, you go into every game with confidence and Liverpool took the game to their hosts with a foul by Andreas Christensen on Sadio Mane, right on the edge of the box, leading to a deserved 14th minute opener.

Mo Salah back-heeled the free-kick, to open up space to the side of Chelsea's defensive wall, for Alexander-Arnold to run onto and the right-back sent a rocket of a shot into the top corner. It was his first goal of the season and what a strike it was. Comparisons aren't always helpful, but the Reds used to have another Scouser in their team by the name of Steven Gerrard who could strike a free-kick like that.

Chelsea had a prime opportunity to level eight minutes later when Tammy Abraham evaded the offside trap to run clean through, but, just like from the penalty spot in the UEFA Super Cup shoot-out in Istanbul, Adrian denied him with a fine save.

The Liverpool goalkeeper couldn't prevent fellow Spaniard Cesar Azpilicueta from scoring moments later following a goalmouth

W

MANAGER: JÜRGEN KLOPP

"It was a really good performance and we scored two wonderful goals. You will never win at Chelsea without putting a proper shift in, and I think we deserved the three points. 15 straight wins is exceptional, but what can I say? We try not to think about it, we just do what we have to do in the next game."

FOR THE RECORD:

Liverpool became the first team in top-flight history to win their opening six matches of a top-flight campaign in two consecutive seasons.

ALSO THIS WEEKEND:

• Manchester City 8-0 Watford
• West Ham United 2-0 Manchester United
• Leicester City 2-1 Tottenham Hotspur

scramble, but VAR spotted Mason Mount offside in the build up and chalked the goal off.

Liverpool made the most of the reprieve. Azpilicueta fouled Gini Wijnaldum on the left flank and Alexander-Arnold rolled the free-kick to Andy Robertson, to again shift the angle. From Robertson's pin-point cross, Roberto Firmino rose almost unchallenged to head the ball home.

It was Firmino's third goal in three away Premier League games and also gave Robertson an assist as he again goes head-to-head with fellow full-back Alexander-Arnold as the pair try to out-do each other when it comes to creating goals.

Had Kepa Arrizabalaga not made an outstanding one-handed save to keep out another Firmino header it would have been game over

shortly after the interval, but Chelsea battled back with N'Golo Kante reducing the deficit 19 minutes from time with a shot from the edge of the box.

A couple of nervy moments followed as Michy Batshuayi and Mount both wasted chances, but with Joel Matip, in particular, defending well and James Milner, Adam Lallana and Joe Gomez all brought on to sure things up, the relentless Reds hung on to make it 15 wins on the spin.

SHEFFIELD UNITED 0
LIVERPOOL 1

Goal: Wijnaldum (70)

28.09.19 • Bramall Lane • Attendance: 31,774
Referee: Anthony Taylor

SHEFFIELD UNITED (5-3-2): D Henderson, Basham, Egan, O'Connell, Baldock, Lundstram, Norwood (C) (Clarke 77), Fleck, Stevens, Robinson (Mousset 60), McBurnie. Subs not used: Moore, Freeman, Jagielka, Osborn, Besic. Booked: O'Connell.

LIVERPOOL (4-3-3): Adrian, Alexander-Arnold, Matip, van Dijk, Robertson, J Henderson (C) (Origi 64), Fabinho, Wijnaldum, Salah, Firmino (Milner 87), Mane (Oxlade-Chamberlain 90). Subs not used: Kelleher, Lovren, Gomez, Lallana. Booked: Adrian.

PRESS BOX:

MOLLY HUDSON, THE TIMES

"You would be hard-pressed to find two managers in the Premier League more passionate on the touchline than Jürgen Klopp and Chris Wilder. The pair are the living embodiments of their clubs. They were like puppets on strings, being yanked this way and that by the actions of their players."

PUNDIT:

JOE COLE, BT SPORT

"This team has got everything. They're fully equipped to win the league and we've seen that today with the performances of van Dijk and Robertson. I put them now as firm favourites because I can see little weaknesses with Man City. With Liverpool you have to trawl through to find half-weaknesses."

SHEFFIELD UNITED v LIVERPOOL

W

MANAGER: JÜRGEN KLOPP
"We were deserved winners. If it's 0-0 we cannot moan and would not. But if there's one winner it should be us. We worked had for it. Winning on days like this is extremely worthy. We scored a lucky goal, we know that. But the boys worked so hard for it."

FOR THE RECORD:
At the fourth time of asking, Bramall Lane became the 55th away ground, out of 57, the Reds have won at in the Premier League. The two that LFC haven't won at are the City Ground (Nottingham Forest, five visits) and Bloomfield Road (Blackpool, one visit).

ALSO THIS WEEKEND:
• Everton 1-3 Manchester City
• Leicester City 5-0 Newcastle United
• Manchester United 1-1 Arsenal

REPORT:
Bramall Lane has long been a bogey ground for Liverpool. A record of three wins in 25 previous visits, scoring only 15 goals, testament to the difficult task the Reds have faced in the Steel City over the years.

In 1978 Bob Paisley's European Champions, fielding a full-strength team, were knocked out of the League Cup at Bramall Lane by the Second Division Blades after missing a host of chances and getting stung by an 80th minute winner. It's not stretching the imagination to say history could have repeated itself in 2019, albeit in the Premier League.

Chris Wilder's side, backed by a partisan crowd relishing their return to the top-flight, were well-organised, defensively dogged and dangerous on the counter-attack. That they prevented Liverpool from having a shot on target until Gini Wijnaldum's 70th minute winner is evidence of how well they played, although the Reds' finishing was partly to blame.

Sadio Mane has been on fire so far this season, but he had a rare off-day in front of goal in Sheffield. Virgil van Dijk's clever pass sent Mane clean through in the 34th minute, but he sliced his effort over. Moments later, a Reds' break started by Wijnaldum, and continued by Mo Salah, ended with Roberto Firmino presenting Mane with another golden opportunity, but this time the foot of the post kept his low shot out.

Adrian pushed an Oliver Norwood attempt wide 20 minutes into the second half and it seemed inevitable that John Fleck would give the Blades the lead when he had time in the box to shoot – only for Andy Robertson to make a flying block. It proved to be the first of two turning points, although had Mane correctly been awarded a penalty after being fouled by John Lundstram there would have been a very different turning point.

Just three minutes after Robertson's block, a cross from substitute Divock Origi was headed out towards Wijnaldum on the edge of the box. The Dutchman volleyed it goalwards. Goalkeeper Dean Henderson, on loan from Manchester United, was perfectly positioned to gather the ball, but allowed it to slip through both his gloves and legs like a greasy chip butty. He could only look on in horror as it trickled over the goalline, sending the travelling Kop behind him wild.

Keeper Henderson did prevent Salah from adding a second when he raced clean through, but with Joel Matip outstanding at the back, and Fabinho protecting his defenders magnificently, the Blades' race was run and the bogey-busting European Champions headed home over the Pennines with Liverpool's first-ever Premier League win at Bramall Lane.

W

LIVERPOOL 2
LEICESTER CITY 1

Goals: Mane (40), Milner (90pen); Maddison (80)
05.10.19 • Anfield • **Attendance:** 53,322
Referee: Chris Kavanagh

LIVERPOOL (4-3-3): Adrian, Alexander-Arnold, Lovren, van Dijk, Robertson, Wijnaldum (Henderson 78), Fabinho, Milner (C), Salah (Lallana 90), Mane, Firmino (Origi 78).
Subs not used: Kelleher, Keita, Gomez, Elliott.
Booked: Fabinho.

LEICESTER CITY (4-1-4-1): Schmeichel (C), Ricardo, Evans, Söyüncü, Chilwell, Ndidi, Barnes (Albrighton 46), Praet (Perez 73), Maddison (Choudhury 86), Tielemans, Vardy.
Subs not used: Ward, Justin, Morgan, Gray.
Booked: Ndidi, Söyüncü, Evans, Choudhury.

PRESS BOX:
PAUL WILSON, THE GUARDIAN
"The Foxes lived up to their billing by giving Liverpool their biggest scare of the domestic season so far. Though Liverpool led for much of the game Klopp was right to feel the encounter might prove difficult. Leicester are third in the table for a reason, and Liverpool were pushed all the way by a side playing a similarly high-energy, in-your-face sort of game."

PUNDIT:
ROBERTO DI MATTEO, BEIN SPORTS
"Choudhury looks like he has used excessive force in that tackle. You can do a tactical foul, which breaks up the play, but look at the speed he gets into him [Mo Salah]. The speed he gets into him, it's dangerous."

MANAGER: JÜRGEN KLOPP
"It was a super game. We upped the tempo. The football we played was so important. Leicester's goal really stopped us, but then we wanted to go forwards. The penalty was obviously a penalty. Milner held his nerve and that was superb. We deserved three points."

FOR THE RECORD:
Liverpool's eight point lead is the largest after eight games since Manchester United led Everton by eight points in 1985/86. United finished fourth that year, Liverpool as champions.

ALSO THIS WEEKEND:
• Manchester City 0-2 Wolverhampton Wanderers
• Newcastle United 1-0 Manchester United
• Burnley 1-0 Everton

REPORT:
The celebrations that greeted James Milner's nervelessly converted 95th minute penalty encapsulated how important a victory it felt like this was. Liverpool supporters erupted when the ball hit the net, whistled Leicester's players in possession for the final couple of minutes like it was a Champions League semi-final, and were treated to Jürgen Klopp's first 'fist-pumps' celebration of the season at full-time.

Not only did that unbridled joy reflect the admiration in how the Reds had dug out another three points when it seemed like two had been lost, it was due recognition for what a good side Liverpool had just beaten.

Brendan Rodgers has galvanised the Foxes since taking charge at the King Power Stadium and it was clear to see, on Rodgers' first return to Anfield as a visiting manager, why Klopp had tipped them to finish in the top three. They press, they run, they play football and with players like Jamie Vardy, Youri Tielemans and goalscorer James

Maddison, they have genuine quality.

But then Liverpool do all those things better than anyone else and in man-of-the-match Sadio Mane have a player that Lionel Messi, judging by his FIFA Player of the Year vote, regards as the best in the world.

Leicester couldn't cope with Mane and it was no surprise that he broke the deadlock in the 40th minute. The Reds beat Leicester's high-press to work a goal-kick to the evergreen James Milner, who played an outstanding pass behind Jonny Evans for Mane to chase. He took the ball in his stride and even though Kasper Schmeichel performed the splits to try to block Mane's low shot, the ball nestled in the Kop-end net. It was Sadio's 50th Premier League goal for LFC in his 100th game.

Mane, after a brilliant double one-two with Mo Salah, hit the side-netting after the break, but Leicester remained in the game and not long after Adrian denied Vardy when he tried to go around him, Maddison fired home an

equaliser after being slipped in by substitute Ayoze Perez.

Fellow Foxes sub Hamza Choudhury then forced Salah off with an ankle injury after a late challenge that left Klopp furious when only a yellow card was brandished, but the drama wasn't over with Leicester's other sub involved in the decisive moment.

Marc Albrighton tackled Divock Origi, but as the ball rolled back into the Leicester box Mane reacted quickest to gather possession. Albrighton challenged again, but this time clipped Mane's ankle and referee Chris Kavanagh pointed to the spot. Rodgers later claimed it was "soft," but then a week earlier Mane hadn't been awarded a clear penalty at Sheffield United and there was far less furore surrounding that.

Up stepped Milner to calmly stroke the ball home and the value of that winner was magnified 24 hours later when Manchester City lost at home to Wolves. It's almost as if a jubilant Anfield sensed it was coming...

MANCHESTER UNITED 1
LIVERPOOL 1

Goals: Rashford (36); Lallana (85)

20.10.19 • Old Trafford • Attendance: 73,737
Referee: Martin Atkinson

MANCHESTER UNITED (3-4-1-2): de Gea, Lindelof, Maguire, Rojo, Wan-Bissaka, McTominay, Fred, Young (C), Pereira (Williams 90), James, Rashford (Martial 84).
Subs not used: Romero, Jones, Mata, Greenwood, Garner.

LIVERPOOL (4-3-3): Alisson, Alexander-Arnold, Matip, van Dijk, Robertson, Henderson (C) (Lallana 71), Fabinho, Wijnaldum (Keita 82), Mane, Firmino, Origi (Oxlade-Chamberlain 60).
Subs not used: Adrian, Lovren, Milner, Gomez.
Booked: Fabinho.

PRESS BOX:

MATT DICKINSON, THE TIMES
"This turned out to be a decent point for Liverpool given how poor they were in the first half, and the range of options to help them get out of a hole was a reminder of just how Jürgen Klopp is is going to have to be clever in deploying resources between now and May to stay ahead of rivals as potent as Manchester City."

PUNDIT:

PETER WALTON, EX-PREMIER LEAGUE REFEREE
"Marcus Rashford's goal should have been overturned because of a clear foul by Victor Lindelof on Divock Origi at the start of the build-up. The VAR process when checking a goal is to go back to see whether the team who have scored obtained the ball in a fair manner, which United did not."

REPORT:

Encounters between Liverpool and Manchester United have had everything over the years, but at Old Trafford there was a new factor to throw into the cauldron: VAR.

Video Assisted Refereeing directly influenced the outcome of this clash on a day when Liverpool didn't play well and lost both their 100% record and the opportunity to match Manchester City's top-flight record of 18 consecutive wins, but showed character to maintain an unbeaten Premier League run that stretches back to January.

The travelling Kop arrived in Manchester with inflatable European Cups and number sixes – a number also printed on placards – to remind their hosts that a sixth European Cup now resides at Anfield.

That European Champions status evidently hadn't gone unnoticed by United boss Ole Gunnar Sólksjaer either as he switched to a 3-4-1-2 formation with the emphasis on trying to stifle Liverpool's full-backs and play on the counter-attack. In truth, Liverpool, who had Divock Origi in for the injured Mo Salah, found it difficult to break United down and in the 36th minute a United counter-attack led to the opening goal.

Victor Lindelof fouled Origi to win possession, but referee Martin Atkinson allowed play to continue. Daniel James broke down the right wing and crossed for Marcus Rashford to touch the ball past Alisson, who was making his first start since recovering from injury. There was a delay while VAR official David Coote studied Lindelof's

MANAGER: JÜRGEN KLOPP

"They scored a goal which shows all the problems with VAR. Mr Atkinson let the game run I'm sure because there is VAR. For me it was a clear foul. VAR looks and says 'you decided like this'. But it was a foul."

FOR THE RECORD:

Adam Lallana's goal was the 28th scored in the final 15 minutes of Premier League games by Liverpool players since the start of 2018/19. No other side has scored more.

ALSO THIS WEEKEND:

• Crystal Palace 0-2 Manchester City
• Tottenham Hotspur 1-1 Watford
• Sheffield United 1-1 Arsenal

foul, but he opted not to overrule his senior colleague, much to Klopp's annoyance.

Two minutes before half-time Sadio Mane equalised after getting in behind Lindelof to take Trent Alexander-Arnold's pass in his stride and finish, but this time VAR did intervene after spotting the ball had brushed the Senegalese speedster's arm as he controlled it. Liverpool remained behind.

The Reds dominated possession after the interval but struggled to create until the arrival of substitutes Alex Oxlade-Chamberlain, Adam Lallana and Naby Keita gave them a different dimension. It was one of that trio who levelled matters with 85 minutes on the clock.

United had 10 men behind the ball when Keita slipped a pass wide

to Andy Robertson, who sent a low cross into the penalty area. With Marcos Rojo preoccupied by pushing Roberto Firmino and Harry Maguire manhandling Mane, the ball was allowed to reach the far post where the unmarked Lallana gleefully tapped it in. It was Lallana's first goal since May 2017 and Robertson's 19th Premier League assist for LFC.

Old Trafford fell silent, with the exception of 3,000 travelling Kopites in the corner, and Liverpool almost snatched all three points late on when Oxlade-Chamberlain's low left-footed snapshot from 20 yards out beat David de Gea, but flashed just past the post.

So Liverpool returned to Merseyside with their 100% record ended, but could feel aggrieved that VAR didn't intervene when it should have.

LIVERPOOL v TOTTENHAM HOTSPUR

LIVERPOOL 2
TOTTENHAM HOTSPUR 1

Goals: Henderson (52), Salah (75pen); Kane (1)
27.10.19 • Anfield • Attendance: 53,222
Referee: Anthony Taylor

LIVERPOOL (4-3-3): Alisson, Alexander-Arnold, Lovren, van Dijk, Robertson, Henderson (C), Fabinho, Wijnaldum (Milner 77), Salah (Gomez 85), Firmino (Origi 90), Mane.
Subs not used: Adrian, Keita, Oxlade-Chamberlain, Lallana.
Booked: Lovren, Alexander-Arnold, Milner.

TOTTENHAM (4-2-3-1): Gazzaniga, Aurier (Moura 84), Alderweireld, Sanchez, Rose, Sissoko, Winks (Ndombele 63), Eriksen (Lo Celso 88), Alli, Son, Kane (C).
Subs not used: Austin, Vertonghen, Dier, Davies. Booked: Sissoko, Rose, Ndombele.

PRESS BOX:
IAN DOYLE, LIVERPOOL ECHO
"Is there a better defensive midfielder in the Premier League than Fabinho? It's a question worth asking after another dominant performance from the Brazilian saw him strengthen his claim of being Liverpool's most consistent performer. He was everywhere."

PUNDIT:
JAMIE CARRAGHER, SKY SPORTS
"Trent Alexander-Arnold is the most creative player for the European Champions and he's 21 playing full-back. That's something you might speak about Dani Alves when he was at Barcelona. Five or six times he's playing 60, 70-yard passes across the pitch. He's one of the best young players in the world. He's something special."

MANAGER: JÜRGEN KLOPP
"I really liked the way we played against really tough opponents. It was a wonderful game of football, it's how you wish games should be. The boys delivered. We had chance after chance and the keeper had sensational save after sensational save. At half-time I said this game had only one problem – the scoreline."

FOR THE RECORD:
Mo Salah's penalty was the 23rd awarded in Premier League games between Liverpool and Tottenham, the most in the history of the competition.

ALSO THIS WEEKEND:
• Southampton 0-9 Leicester City
• Brighton & Hove Albion 3-2 Everton
• Manchester City 3-0 Aston Villa

REPORT:

Twenty-one seconds into the 2019 Champions League final between Liverpool and Tottenham Hotspur in Madrid, Sadio Mane's cross was blocked by the raised arm of Moussa Sissoko in the Spurs penalty area. The referee blew for a spot-kick and Mo Salah struck the ball into the net 86 seconds later.

Fast forward to Anfield a little under five months on and the tables were turned. Forty-seven seconds into this Premier League encounter Harry Kane stooped to head Tottenham into the lead after Heung-Min Son's shot deflected off Dejan Lovren and struck the frame of the goal. It was a slap in the face, but boy did the Reds recover.

Liverpool were brilliant. They tore into Tottenham with effort, passion, skill and aptitude while refusing to let the visitors' time-wasting tactics – from slowly-taken goal-kicks and throw-ins to conceding numerous free-kicks and stopping them from being taken quickly – frustrate them.

The only problem was they ran into

goalkeeper Paulo Gazzaniga, who was performing like he was Ray Clemence. The Argentinian made 12 saves – the most in a single Premier League game by any goalkeeper for two years – including some first-half worldies.

A full-stretch save from Salah, before blocking Roberto Firmino from the rebound, was outstanding. Another full-length plunge kept out a Trent Alexander-Arnold piledriver from Andy Robertson's pull-back, and there was a flying tip-over to deny Virgil van Dijk. Mane also headed a good opportunity wide.

Gazzaniga was at it again after the break, keeping out Firmino twice from close range – once by sitting on the ball on his goalline after it went through his legs – and he also created an opportunity for Spurs to double their lead when launching a long kick downfield, but Son could only drive against the crossbar after rounding Alisson.

Liverpool took full advantage. With 52 minutes on the clock man-of-the-match Fabinho – who was so good at sweeping up everything in midfield that Jürgen Klopp

compared him to a Dyson vacuum cleaner – clipped a lovely pass towards Firmino in the box.

The Brazilian was blatantly shoved in the back by Danny Rose, but while Anfield howled for a penalty Jordan Henderson arrived at the far post and angled a left-footed half-volley back across goal and into the far corner. Finally, the Reds were deservedly level. Now to get a winner.

Salah and Gini Wijnaldum both had efforts saved, but, just like in the last home game against Leicester, it was the endeavour of Mane that proved to be decisive. After pressing Serge Aurier in his own penalty area the Reds forward lost possession, but nicked the ball back just as Aurier was launching his clearance. Instead of connecting with the ball, Aurier booted Mane in the back of both legs to concede a stonewall penalty.

Just like he did in Madrid, up stepped Salah and, although he was facing a different goalkeeper, the outcome was the same. The net rippled, Liverpool went ahead and for Tottenham there was no way back.

ASTON VILLA 1
LIVERPOOL 2

Goals: Trezeguet (21); Robertson (87), Mane (90)
02.11.19 • Villa Park • **Attendance: 41,878**
Referee: Jon Moss

ASTON VILLA (4-2-3-1): Heaton, Guilbert (El Mohamady 69), Engels, Mings (C), Targett, Nakamba, Douglas Luiz, (Hourihane 73), El Ghazi, McGinn, Trezeguet, Wesley (Kodjia 86).
Subs not used: Steer, Taylor, Lansbury, Konsa.
Booked: El Ghazi.

LIVERPOOL (4-3-3): Alisson, Alexander-Arnold, Lovren, van Dijk, Robertson, Henderson (C), Lallana (Keita 84), Wijnaldum (Origi 65), Salah (Oxlade-Chamberlain 65), Firmino, Mane.
Subs not used: Adrian, Fabinho, Milner, Gomez. Booked: Mane, van Dijk.

PRESS BOX:
DAVE ARMITAGE, DAILY MIRROR
"Just as Liverpool's unbeaten start to the season looked in dire straights, up stepped Mane. His cross to the far post for Robertson's 87th minute equaliser was sublime, but his encore was even better. Trent Alexander-Arnold swung a corner towards the near post and Mane crouched to steer home his header from a ridiculous angle."

PUNDIT:
CHRIS KAMARA, GOALS ON SUNDAY
"In my opinion this is made up, this has been made up by somebody at Stockley Park who's decided they don't want this to be a goal. That is my opinion, and that is my honest opinion. From the naked eye you don't need that calibration of dots or whatever to tell you, look at Tyrone Mings' knee – Firmino is onside."

ASTON VILLA v LIVERPOOL

34

W

MANAGER: JÜRGEN KLOPP

"I don't always believe we can win every game, but I never give up. So when we scored the equaliser I thought, 'that's what we deserve'. We know we can do better, but on days like this you just need to be ready to fight. After the first half we realised we were on the wrong path and we made changes."

FOR THE RECORD:

This was Liverpool's 14th consecutive victory against sides newly-promoted to the Premier League with three of those wins coming this season.

ALSO THIS WEEKEND:

• Bournemouth 1-0 Manchester United
• Manchester City 2-1 Southampton
• Everton 1-1 Tottenham Hotspur

REPORT:

On an afternoon when Roberto Firmino had a goal disallowed by VAR due to his armpit being offside, Liverpool won all three points at Villa Park by the skin of their teeth.

With 86 minutes on the clock Dean Smith's resilient Aston Villa side led 1-0 and Liverpool were staring down the barrel of a first Premier League defeat since January. When the final whistle went, the Reds had not only avoided a loss but swerved a points-dropping draw, too. No wonder the scenes in the away end were wilder than when a travelling Kopite kissed Divock Origi after a Villa Park goal in 2016.

Fabinho, a booking away from a one-match suspension, was left on the bench with next weekend's Manchester City game in mind and Adam Lallana came into midfield, but it was Sadio Mane who missed the best early chance, heading Jordan Henderson's clipped cross wide.

It was also Mane that conceded the free-kick Villa scored from, Trezeguet evading Liverpool's high-line to plant the ball home and then avoiding having it chalked off by a VAR review. Roberto Firmino wasn't so fortunate.

The assistant referee's flag went up when the Brazilian tapped home Mane's 28th minute cross, but VAR appeared to show that he was onside. However, the lines were then recalibrated by VAR official Martin Atkinson and the offside decision stood.

Such was the social media furore that followed the Premier League released an official statement, before half-time, to clarify: "Liverpool's Roberto Firmino was flagged offside before putting the ball in the net against Aston Villa and the decision was confirmed by VAR. The red line signifies Firmino and was aligned to his armpit, which was marginally ahead of the last Villa defender." Talk about the pits!

Such a bump in the road would send some teams down the wrong track, but not this Liverpool side. They dominated the second half. Mane forced a fine save from Tom Heaton, substitute Alex Oxlade-Chamberlain forced a fine save from Bjorn Engels (but VAR decided it wasn't handball) and Trent Alexander-Arnold, on his 100th Liverpool appearance, bent a shot narrowly past the upright.

Just when it looked like the goal wouldn't come, Mane curled an 87th minute cross in from the right wing to the far post where Andy Robertson darted in to score the first headed goal of his Liverpool career. And the Reds weren't finished there.

Alexander-Arnold's direct free-kick was deflected over with just a minute of the five allotted stoppage-time minutes to play. The Reds' right-back ran over to take the corner and curled it towards the front post where Mane put his head in where it hurts and sent a glancing header past Heaton. The travelling Kop erupted, Mane was engulfed by his team-mates.

As the players walked off just moments later with all three points secured, Virgil van Dijk spotted an LFCTV camera in the Villa Park tunnel and mouthed: 'That's what we do'.

They do, time and time again.

LIVERPOOL v MANCHESTER CITY

W

LIVERPOOL 3
MANCHESTER CITY 1
Goals: Fabinho (6), Salah (13), Mane (51); B Silva (78)
10.11.19 • Anfield • **Attendance:** 53,324
Referee: Michael Oliver

LIVERPOOL (4-3-3): Alisson, Alexander-Arnold, Lovren, van Dijk, Robertson, Henderson (C) (Milner 61), Fabinho, Wijnaldum, Salah (Gomez 87), Firmino (Oxlade-Chamberlain 79), Mane.
Subs not used: Adrian, Keita, Lallana, Origi.

MANCHESTER CITY (4-2-3-1): Bravo, Walker, Stones, Fernandinho (C), Angelino, Rodri, Gundogan, B Silva, De Bruyne, Sterling, Aguero (Jesus 71).
Subs not used: Carson, D Silva, Mahrez, Cancelo, Otamendi, Foden.
Booked: Rodri, Jesus.

PRESS BOX:
JOHN CROSS, DAILY MIRROR
"What we witnessed at Anfield felt like a seismic shift in the title race. The Reds are now the team to beat with City the underdogs. Liverpool still have to negotiate a fixture backlog – with the Club World Cup and Carabao Cup fiasco looming next month – but it's hard to see anyone stopping them now."

PUNDIT:
JOSE MOURINHO, SKY SPORTS
"I think the team is a complete puzzle. I feel the way they play is adapted to the qualities of the players. City are capable of winning seven, eight, nine matches in a row, but I can't see how Liverpool can lose this advantage of nine points to them."

MANAGER: JÜRGEN KLOPP
"What a game. If you want to win against City you have to do something special and we had to be intense. When City started to control it more in the last 15 minutes, it was tense, but then you saw the quality and what the boys can do. The boys did 75 minutes of unbelievable stuff."

FOR THE RECORD:
Sadio Mane's goal was his 22nd in the league at Anfield since August 2018 – the most by any player at a single venue during the last two seasons.

ALSO THIS WEEKEND:
• Leicester City 2-0 Arsenal
• Chelsea 2-0 Crystal Palace
• Wolverhampton Wanderers 2-1 Aston Villa

→

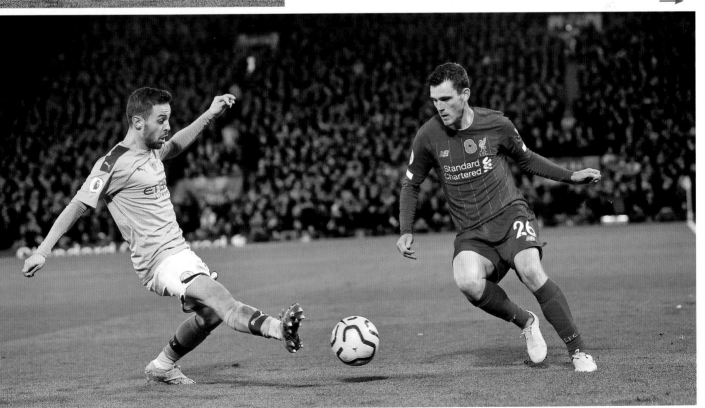

REPORT:

Four years ago, after being appointed as manager of Liverpool Football Club, Jürgen Klopp did a round of media interviews. Everybody remembers his desire to turn Liverpool supporters "from doubter to believer," but there's another quote that seems increasingly prophetic.

"If it's possible, can we be the hardest team to beat in the world?" he said. "Let's try to be this." There's an argument to say his aim has already been achieved.

Before the European champions' heart-pumping 3-1 victory against the English champions, Pep Guardiola was certainly thinking that way. "They're an exceptional team and the stadium makes an influence. The history speaks for itself, it's something special, but I think it's more for the quality of the team and what they do, the quality of the players and the manager they have. I would say, right now, it's the toughest stadium in Europe to go to."

He would know. Liverpool's 3-1 victory was the Manchester City manager's fourth loss at Anfield in five visits – his most defeats at any ground – and means City have now only won twice in front of the Kop in 52 visits since 1956.

The sight of Guardiola remonstrating with fourth official Mike Dean on the touchline, confronting referee Michael Oliver on the pitch at full-time and telling

journalists to ask head of refereeing Mike Riley and his people about VAR at full-time was proof of how the heat of the Anfield battle can get into opponents' heads. It felt like a day when the Reds were taking over, a significant milestone in the Premier League title race.

Guardiola's anger stemmed from an alleged handball by Trent Alexander-Arnold in the sixth minute, although only after the ball had struck Bernardo Silva's hand first. Referee Michael Oliver played on and 22 seconds later Liverpool were ahead when Fabinho controlled Ilkay Gundogan's clearance 25 yards out and fired a rocket of a shot past Claudio Bravo.

Anfield celebrated – a second wave of cheers emerging after VAR gave the goal the green light – and seven minutes later the place was rocking when the Reds scored a goal that was reminiscent of Terry McDermott's famous header in the 7-0 win against Tottenham Hotspur in 1978.

Alexander-Arnold played a glorious left-footed, cross-field pass from right to left that Andy Robertson took in his stride before delivering an angled cross that bounced once before Mo Salah, arriving at speed, met it with his head and planted the ball into the far corner. What. A. Goal.

Alexander-Arnold's initial pass took six City players out and Robertson's cross went past the entire back four before Salah reached it. Liverpool have never had a more creative pair of full-backs.

City looked stunned, but they'd not racked up 198 points during the last two seasons by accident and, after regaining their composure, created chances with Alisson denying Sergio Aguero and Kevin de Bruyne, while a deflected Angelino cross clipped the outside of the post. A City goal could have been a game-changer, but instead the Redmen went further ahead.

Seven minutes into the second half, Jordan Henderson burst past Gundogan and Angelino on the right before delivering a deep cross to the far post that the diving Sadio Mane met with his head. Bravo got a hand to the ball, but could only push it into the net. Game, set and match.

Bernardo Silva pulled one back in the 78th minute – much to the annoyance of Klopp, who had been trying to make a substitution just seconds earlier only for referee Oliver to allow the game to restart – and had another penalty shout turned down when Raheem Sterling's cross hit Alexander-Arnold's hand at close range.

Sterling, who again failed to score on an Anfield return, then clashed with Joe Gomez – a set-to that would continue on international duty the following day – as tempers threatened to boil over in this increasingly tempestuous rivalry. Ultimately, Liverpool deservedly emerged with all three points to increase the gap over City to nine points.

Perhaps the image of the day, however, came at full-time when Klopp posed for a photograph with Sean Cox, who was attending his first Anfield game since being left in a coma by the Roma fans who attacked him before the 2018 Champions League semi-final.

In the 18 months since Liverpool have remained undefeated at Anfield in the Premier League and Champions League. Manchester City will tell you there isn't a harder team to beat in the world.

CRYSTAL PALACE 1
LIVERPOOL 2

Goals: Zaha (82); Mane (49), Firmino (85)

23.11.19 • Selhurst Park • Attendance: 25,486

Referee: Kevin Friend

CRYSTAL PALACE (4-5-1): Guaita, Ward (Kelly 70), Tomkins, Cahill, van Aanholt, Townsend, Kouyate (Schlupp 72), Milivojevic (C), McArthur, Zaha, J Ayew (Benteke 76). Subs not used: Hennessey, Dann, Meyer, McCarthy.

LIVERPOOL (4-3-3): Alisson, Alexander-Arnold, Lovren, van Dijk, Robertson, Henderson (C) (Milner 79), Fabinho, Wijnaldum, Mane, Firmino (Gomez 89), Oxlade-Chamberlain (Origi 64). Subs not used: Adrian, Keita, Salah, Lallana. Booked: Fabinho

PRESS BOX:

IAN DOYLE, LIVERPOOL ECHO

"No team in history has ever taken more top-flight points than the 37 Liverpool have accrued from a possible 39 so far this campaign. The Reds extended their unbeaten league run to 30 games, one short of the club record set back in 1988."

PUNDIT:

ALAN SHEARER, BBC MATCH OF THE DAY

"This Liverpool team don't do defeats. They keep on going and came back straight at them. In the last five minutes, again, Firmino is there and he tucks it away. Again, Liverpool didn't play particularly well, but they got the right result due to the desire they had."

REPORT:

To understand how Liverpool won this tricky, post-international break fixture at Selhurst Park then you need look no further than captain Jordan Henderson.

While rival supporters claimed Liverpool were lucky to have won yet another game with a goal in the last five minutes – Roberto Firmino's winner meant the Reds had secured eight points this season in the final five minutes – skipper Hendo had a completely different take on the matter.

"I've heard a lot in recent months about 'luck' playing a part in some of the wins we've managed this season. My personal view is it is the professionalism of this squad and the dedication to what we are looking to achieve that delivers the so-called luck. Only hard work and the highest standards allow the sort of moments we enjoyed

in London to happen. Without that, the so-called luck is completely irrelevant."

With Mo Salah only fit enough to sit on the bench due to an ankle problem, Andy Robertson also struggling with an ankle knock, Sadio Mane suffering an injury playing for Senegal and Alisson, Fabinho and Roberto Firmino only arriving back from Brazilian international duty in Abu Dhabi 48 hours earlier, it was understandable that Liverpool weren't at their best.

Jordan Ayew missed the best early chance, diverting Cheikhou Kouyate's cross wide, before James Tomkins headed the Eagles in front in the 42nd minute only for VAR to rule the goal out for a push by Ayew on Dejan Lovren. That Palace boss Roy Hodgson later admitted he agreed with the decision was indicative of how clear-cut

MANAGER: JÜRGEN KLOPP

"Today, I have no problem that we were not brilliant because in a game like this you just have to make sure you're ready to fight for the result and we were that from the first minute. Getting a result at Crystal Palace, you never take for granted. So, it feels good."

FOR THE RECORD:

Sadio Mane scored in his fifth consecutive game against Crystal Palace, the joint best run by a Liverpool player against a Premier League opponent alongside Michael Owen (v Newcastle) and Luis Suarez (v Norwich).

ALSO THIS WEEKEND:
• Manchester City 2-1 Chelsea
• Everton 0-2 Norwich City
• Sheffield United 3-3 Manchester United

it was, no matter what the pundits said.

Mane skimmed a shot just wide of the post from Henderson's through-ball shortly after the interval, but it wasn't long until he chalked up his eighth goal against Palace. Liverpool won possession in midfield, worked the ball out to Robertson on the left and, from his cross, Mane struck a bouncing left-footed effort that went into the net via Vicente Guaita's right glove and both posts.

Andros Townsend stung Alisson's palms, Guaita saved from Firmino and ex-Red Christian Benteke, on as a sub, sent a scissor-kick wide of the post as both sides created chances before Wilfried Zaha conjured up an 82nd minute equaliser. The winger allowed Townsend's pass to run across his body before firing a low shot into the bottom corner.

It looked like that would be enough to earn the hosts a draw, but Liverpool yet again found away to take all three points. Virgil van Dijk met Trent Alexander-Arnold's 85th minute corner and, following a scramble in the six-yard box, the ball fell to Firmino, who side-footed it home.

Zaha missed a late chance to equalise, albeit from a suspiciously-looking offside position, in front of the Holmesdale Road end while in the far corner of the Arthur Wait Stand the travelling Kop celebrated another hard-fought three points from an encounter that was every bit as tricky as it looked likely to be.

LIVERPOOL 2
BRIGHTON & HOVE ALBION 1

Goals: Van Dijk (18, 24); Dunk (79)

30.11.19 • Anfield • Attendance: 53,319
Referee: Martin Atkinson

LIVERPOOL (4-3-3): Alisson, Alexander-Arnold, Lovren, van Dijk, Robertson, Oxlade-Chamberlain (Adrian 78), Henderson (C), Wijnaldum, Salah (Lallana 69), Firmino (76), Mane. Subs not used: Milner, Keita, Gomez, Shaqiri. Sent off: Alisson

BRIGHTON & HOVE ALBION (4-5-1): Ryan, Montoya (Alzate 69), Webster, Dunk (C), Burn, Gross, Propper, Stephens, Bissouma (Trossard 69), Mooy, Connolly (Maupay 76). Subs not used: Button, Duffy, Murray, Schelotto.

LIVERPOOL v BRIGHTON & HOVE ALBION

REPORT:

Liverpool supporters on the Kop spent the opening six minutes waving Hillsborough banners and chanting 'Justice for the 96' in solidarity for the 96 following the 'not guilty' verdict in the David Duckenfield trial 48 hours earlier, so it was somewhat fitting that both Reds' goals came within six minutes of this 2-1 win.

Virgil van Dijk was the man responsible for both, twice heading Trent Alexander-Arnold set-pieces into the Anfield Road end net. It was the first time any Premier League player has scored with two headers in such a short space of time since van Dijk did the same against Watford nine months earlier.

Yet despite both goals being created and scored by Reds' defenders, Liverpool have failed to keep a clean sheet at Anfield all season. Bizarrely, the Reds have conceded one goal in each of their seven home league games and have now won seven of their 14 league games by a scoreline of 2-1. No wonder van Dijk said afterwards "we are in a good position points-wise, but we know we can do maybe that extra 10% still."

Liverpool created six good chances during the first half with van Dijk's headers, the first from an Alexander-Arnold free-kick and the second from an Alexander-Arnold corner, putting daylight between the two teams. Had the Seagulls' Mat Ryan not produced a string of saves from Roberto Firmino (twice), Sadio Mane and Alex Oxlade-Chamberlain, the contest would have been over by half-time.

Alisson had palmed a Davy Propper shot away in the first half, but when he did the same to deny Leandro Trossard in the 78th minute he was outside of his penalty area. The red card that followed was inevitable.

Not since Sander Westerveld, against Everton in 1999, had a Reds' keeper been dismissed at Anfield. Adrian was summoned from the bench, replacing Oxlade-Chamberlain, but was still lining up his wall when Brighton skipper Lewis Dunk took the free-kick quickly and rolled the ball into the unguarded corner of the net, setting up a nervy finale.

Without the injured (and suspended) Fabinho to protect the back four, Jordan Henderson did a fine job in that role, while Andy Robertson was magnificent on the left, but Adrian had to push out Aaron Mooy's low shot and then scramble to keep out Pascal Gross to deny Brighton an equaliser.

The heartfelt cheers when the full-time whistle eventually blew – Liverpool equalling the club record of 31 league games unbeaten in the process – was evidence of just how important the Anfield crowd felt holding on to all three points could be.

It may not have been as comfortable as Jürgen Klopp would like, but having the willingness and desire to keep fighting when things go against you is an admirable quality to possess. Hopefully it also gave the Hillsborough families and survivors, who have displayed those qualities and more for the last 30 years, some comfort at the end of a difficult week.

PRESS BOX:
PAUL JOYCE, THE TIMES
"While Klopp will admire his players' appetite for self-improvement, he is also quick to recognise their evolution means victories can also come in different guises. How Liverpool win is not defined by one style, but, in the league, winning is all they do."

PUNDIT:
PHIL NEVILLE, BBC MATCH OF THE DAY
"When you see a team at the top of the league you look at the qualities that they have that can help them win the title. Sometimes they can blitz a team like Liverpool do, today they had to dig in deep because Brighton had 55% possession and controlled the game for long periods."

MANAGER: JÜRGEN KLOPP
"I'm really happy and proud of the desire the boys showed. The red card made it a really special win, to be honest. It was difficult this game because Brighton are a good football side. They had a lot of possession and we had to work really hard. I loved that the boys were prepared to do that after a busy week."

FOR THE RECORD:
Adrian became the first ever goalkeeper to come on as a substitute in two league games in Liverpool FC history.

ALSO THIS WEEKEND:
• Newcastle United 2-2 Manchester City
• Chelsea 0-1 West Ham United
• Leicester City 2-1 Everton

LIVERPOOL v EVERTON

LIVERPOOL 5
EVERTON 2

Goals: Origi (6, 31), Shaqiri (17), Mane (45), Wijnaldum (90); Keane (21), Richarlison (45)

04.12.19 • Anfield • **Attendance: 53,094**

Referee: Mike Dean

LIVERPOOL (4-3-3): Adrian, Alexander-Arnold (Gomez 83), Lovren, van Dijk, Robertson, Lallana (Henderson 72), Wijnaldum, Milner (C), Shaqiri, Origi (Firmino 73), Mane.
Subs not used: Kelleher, Keita, Oxlade-Chamberlain, Salah.
Booked: Alexander-Arnold.

EVERTON (5-4-1): Pickford, Sidibie (Bernard 35), Holgate, Keane, Mina, Digne, Iwobi, Davies (Schneiderlin 72), Sigurdsson (C), Richarlison, Calvert-Lewin (Kean 60).
Subs not used: Lossl, Baines, Walcott, Tosun. Booked: Richarlison, Davies.

PRESS BOX:

PAUL GORST, LIVERPOOL ECHO

"'Merry Christmas Everton' rung around the Kop as Origi celebrated another goal against the Toffees. With three of the last four Decembers turning up defeats to Liverpool, Blues fans must be sick to the back teeth of that particular ditty."

PUNDIT:

THIERRY HENRY, AMAZON PRIME

"What's going to be important for Divock Origi now, is that he played in the middle. That's a great sign of respect for the work he is doing from Jürgen Klopp. What you saw tonight is him making those runs from the middle to the right because he's comfortable on the wing."

REPORT:

The Official Liverpool FC Matchday Programme featured an interview with Divock Origi ahead of the 234th Merseyside derby in which he was asked about scoring against Everton at Anfield in 2016, 2017 and 2018.

"I don't know why that is!" he replied. "I feel like it is just very big moments for me. I thrive off the energy in the good games, the big games, but this doesn't mean I will score in every derby! The most important thing is to win the game, but if I can score against Everton again then why not?"

Why not indeed, as it took Origi just six minutes to add 2019 to his list of Anfield goals against the Blues. The Belgian was selected to play through the middle with Sadio Mane on the left and Xherdan Shaqiri brought in on the right. It perhaps wasn't the front three that

Everton were expecting to face and they simply couldn't cope with their pace and movement.

Origi's opener came from a slide-rule Sadio Mane pass. He darted between Michael Keane and Yerry Mina, touched the ball past Jordan Pickford – who had rushed off his goalline – and rolled the ball into the empty net.

A little over 10 minutes later Mane was at it again, this time slipping a pass in behind the Blues' defence to pick out a diagonal run from Shaqiri, who slid the ball across Pickford and into the net.

Everton looked in trouble, but got a goal back in the 21st minute when Alex Iwobi's cross deflected off Dejan Lovren to Michael Keane, who lifted the ball over Adrian.

Lovren was involved in the next goal too, but this time with a pass

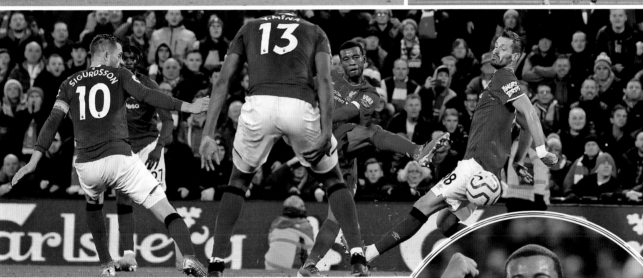

MANAGER: JÜRGEN KLOPP:
"All the goals were incredible, outstanding. Wonderful goals, sensational passes, super pieces of football. I loved it a lot! We needed fresh legs and I had to show my respect to the boys in the squad, that's all. They proved it. It is much more fun making changes, all of the boys are ready to deliver performances like this."

FOR THE RECORD:
This was the first time Liverpool had scored five against Everton since a 5-0 win at Goodison Park in 1982 and the first time they had done so at Anfield since 1965.

ALSO THIS MIDWEEK:
• Burnley 1-4 Manchester City
• Leicester City 2-0 Watford
• Manchester United 2-1 Tottenham Hotspur

that took out the entire Everton defence. Origi ran in behind them, allowed the ball to drop over his shoulder, controlled it with the kind of touch you'd associate with Thierry Henry in his prime and lofted it – using his instep – over the outstretched arms of Pickford.

It was a goal of pure beauty, and one that meant only Steven Gerrard and Robbie Fowler have netted more Premier League goals for the Reds in Merseyside derbies than Origi. Which is quite remarkable given this was only his sixth derby.

Liverpool's fourth goal was a breathtaking counter-attack from an Everton corner. Mane led the charge and sent Trent Alexander-Arnold sprinting away down the left wing. As Tom Davies came across to meet him, Alexander-Arnold slipped the ball back inside to Mane, who planted it into the bottom corner with a first-time, left-footed finish from outside the penalty area. The cheer that greeted

it was so loud they could probably hear it at Michael Buble's gig being held at the M&S Bank Arena at the same time.

Not since 1935 had Liverpool scored four first-half goals against Everton, but a momentary lapse of concentration in stoppage time allowed Richarlison to reduce the deficit with a diving header.

The second half didn't quite live up to the first. Marco Silva's side battened down the hatches with Mane, who curled a shot inches wide, coming closest to scoring until the 90th minute. Substitute Roberto Firmino twisted his way past Mason Holgate before pulling the ball back for Gini Wijnaldum to fire into the bottom corner.

It was a fitting way to complete Jürgen Klopp's 100th victory in the Premier League and allowed Liverpool supporters to bounce into work and school early the following morning – probably at five-to…

BOURNEMOUTH 0
LIVERPOOL 3

Goals: Oxlade-Chamberlain (35), Keita (44), Salah (54)
07.12.19 • Vitality Stadium • Attendance: 10,832
Referee: Chris Kavanagh

BOURNEMOUTH (4-4-2): Ramsdale, Francis (C), Mepham, Ake (Simpson 35), Rico, Groeneveld, Lerma, Billing (L Cook 58), Fraser, Solanke, C Wilson (Gosling 64).
Subs not used: Boruc, Surman, Ibe, Stacey.

LIVERPOOL (4-3-3): Alisson, Gomez, Lovren (Alexander-Arnold 40), van Dijk, Robertson (Jones 76), Keita, Henderson (C), Milner, Salah, Firmino, Oxlade-Chamberlain (Shaqiri 87).
Subs not used: Adrian, Mane, Origi, Elliott.
Booked: Gomez

PRESS BOX:
JIM WHITE, DAILY TELEGRAPH
"As the rest of the Premier League huffs and puffs in their wake, this was not just another win for Jürgen Klopp's points-gathering machine, at times it was so comfortable it appeared as if his players were wearing slippers."

PUNDIT:
PAUL MERSON,
SKY SOCCER SATURDAY
"Liverpool made it look like an FA Cup third-round game against a League Two or a non-league team. That's no disrespect to Bournemouth, but that's how Liverpool made them look. They were head and shoulders above – so, so comfortable."

MANAGER: JÜRGEN KLOPP
"For the boys, that was the most used word in the dressing-room when I came in, 'clean sheet, clean sheet, clean sheet'. Everybody was desperate for that and now we have it, so let's have it more often. I forgot actually how it feels, to be honest. It's great."

FOR THE RECORD:
Mo Salah scored in his fifth consecutive game against Bournemouth on his 100th Premier League appearance. He's netted more goals against the Cherries (7) than any other club.

ALSO THIS WEEKEND:
• Manchester City 1-2 Manchester United
• Aston Villa 1-4 Leicester City
• Tottenham Hotspur 5-0 Burnley

REPORT:
For a team riding high in the Premier League it seemed like a statistical anomaly, but when the Reds travelled to the South Coast to take on Bournemouth they did so having failed to keep a clean sheet for 13 consecutive matches in all competitions.

Due to injuries, a suspension for Alisson and the Carabao Cup, three different goalkeepers had played during that time while Virgil van Dijk had lined up alongside three different central defenders. Perhaps such disruption was an underlying factor. More likely it was a combination of several other things, but you could sense at the Vitality Stadium that it was a run Liverpool's players were determined to end. And they did.

Describing this as a routine away win does a disservice to the effort the players put in, but there can be no doubting that Jürgen Klopp's side made their 3-0 victory look comfortable. The Cherries failed to muster a single shot on target while the Reds had 21 efforts on goal. If you were being picky, they should really have scored more.

Neither Alex Oxlade-Chamberlain nor Naby Keita had scored in the Premier League this season, but by half-time they had become the

15th and 16th different Liverpool players to write their names on the scoresheet in league games.

Bournemouth's Nathan Ake was forced off with a hamstring injury in the 35th minute and he had barely left the pitch when Oxlade-Chamberlain put Liverpool ahead. Jordan Henderson picked the forward-running midfielder out with an exquisite pass and he nudged the ball past Aaron Ramsdale on the volley. It was the Ox's first Premier League goal since January 2018, although there was a change in central defence of our own five minutes later when Dejan Lovren was substituted due to injury.

Keita added the second shortly before half-time with a flicked finish, using the outside of his right boot, following an outstanding piece of creativity from Mo Salah. The Egyptian controlled the ball on the edge of the box before back-heeling it past three defenders to play Keita in. It was one of the assists of the season.

Ramsdale prevented Keita from scoring again after the interval when he clutched the Guinea international's low volley, so Liverpool's no.8 made a goal instead.

Intercepting a stray ball from Jack Simpson, he threaded a pass between a couple of Bournemouth defenders that Salah latched onto before turning the ball into the net.

That was Salah's fifth goal from his three away appearances against Eddie Howe's side, having now scored in each of his visits to the Vitality Stadium as a Liverpool player. He would have struck an sixth had Ramsdale not dived to palm his rising drive away.

Curtis Jones came on for his Premier League debut, but as Klopp admitted afterwards it was the clean sheet that the players celebrated the most. Sometimes all you need is one for others to follow...

LIVERPOOL 2
WATFORD 0

Goals: Salah (38, 90)

14.12.19 • Anfield • Attendance: 53,311

Referee: Andre Marriner

LIVERPOOL (4-2-3-1): Alisson, Alexander-Arnold, Gomez, van Dijk, Milner, Henderson (C), Wijnaldum (Robertson 59), Shaqiri (Oxlade-Chamberlain 70), Firmino (Origi 88), Mane, Salah. Subs not used: Adrian, Keita, Lallana, Williams. Booked: Henderson, Milner.

WATFORD (4-2-3-1): Foster, Mariappa, Kabasele, Cathcart, Femenia, Capoue, Hughes, Sarr, Doucoure (Quina 87), Deulofeu, Deeney (C) (Gray 75). Subs not used: Gomes, Dawson, Chalobah, Success, Foulquier. Booked: Hughes

PRESS BOX:
OLIVER HOLT, SUNDAY TIMES
"When Liverpool kicked off against Watford, Anfield was still agog with the news that Klopp had signed a new extended contract that will keep him at the club until 2024, reassuring supporters that the glories the German boss has restored will not melt away again just as Liverpool's hegemony in English football appears to have been re-established."

PUNDIT:
MATTHEW SYED, THE TIMES
"I am not a Liverpool fan, but can I be honest? I love that Jürgen Klopp has signed a four-and-a-half year extension with this great club. I love the fact that he lives and breathes Liverpool. Above all, I love the fact that we might be about to witness something that is often absent in this promiscuous, globalised world: a dynasty."

LIVERPOOL v WATFORD

50

MANAGER: JÜRGEN KLOPP

"It was not the prettiest game, but I am more than happy with that. At this stage you have to show resilience and I believe we did that today. We have so many games but we are happy with this. Watford had their chances, but we scored ours."

FOR THE RECORD:

Liverpool became the first team since Sunderland in 1891/92 – the season before LFC was formed – to win 16 consecutive top-flight games while scoring at least twice.

ALSO THIS WEEKEND:

• Leicester City 1-1 Norwich City
• Chelsea 0-1 Bournemouth
• Arsenal 0-3 Manchester City

REPORT:

Anfield legend has it that when Bill Shankly was Liverpool manager, the Spion Kop would suck the ball into the back of the net. So maybe it was fate that, to mark the 60th anniversary of Shanks' appointment, the great man was on the front of the official matchday programme on an afternoon when the Kop seemed to blow out a couple of Watford chances.

Under the management of Nigel Pearson for the first time, the visitors belied their bottom-of-the-table league position with a solid first half display. On a blustery afternoon they made things difficult for the Reds and were unfortunate to go into the half-time interval a goal down.

Mo Salah broke the deadlock in the 38th minute following a lightning-quick counter-attack from a Watford corner. Gini Wijnaldum cleared at the near post, Roberto Firmino sent Sadio Mane away down the left and he in turn played Salah through.

Kiko Femenia came across to meet him, but Salah turned back past the full-back and, with the ball on his right foot, brilliantly curled it past Ben Foster into the far corner. It was an outstanding finish to a clinical move.

A minute before that goal Abdoulaye Doucoure had a glorious chance to score, but mis-kicked in front of goal, and just a minute afterwards Ismaila Sarr did exactly the same. Gerard Deulofeu's low shot was parried by Alisson, but the ball fell to Sarr just eight yards from goal.

An equaliser looked inevitable, but instead of smashing it into the net the Senegalese forward somehow sliced it behind himself. "I'm pretty sure this time I can say the wind helped us," was Jürgen Klopp's take on the matter.

Had it been the 1960s you can bet Shankly would have claimed the Kop blew the ball off Sarr's foot, and he might have had something to say about VAR disallowing a brilliant Mane header, from Xherdan Shaqiri's whipped-in cross, five minutes into the second half. Whether it was his armpit or hip that deemed to be offside was unclear, but it's for such reasons why Klopp – who signed a new four-and-a-half contract the day before this game – says he no longer celebrates goals. Defenders now get the benefit of the doubt.

Two early second half saves from Alisson should not be underestimated in terms of importance, while the loss of Wijnaldum to a hamstring injury was a blow. Both Salah and Firmino also failed to make the most of further chances that came their way, but it was the Egyptian King who confirmed Liverpool's club-record unbeaten league run would extend to a 34th game.

Mane escaped down the right and although substitute Divock Origi miscued his shot from the pull-back, the ball fell to Salah, who nutmegged Christian Kabasele on the goalline with an audacious back-heel flick.

It was his 84th goal for the Reds – two more than Luis Suarez managed having played seven less games – and sent Liverpool to Qatar for the FIFA Club World Cup 10 points clear at the top of the Premier League.

LEICESTER CITY v LIVERPOOL

LEICESTER CITY 0
LIVERPOOL 4

Goals: Firmino (31, 74), Milner (71pen),
Alexander-Arnold (78)

26.12.19 • King Power Stadium •
Attendance: 32,211 • Referee: Michael Oliver

PRESS BOX:

BARNEY RONAY, THE GUARDIAN
"Trent Alexander-Arnold is something else, a 21-year-old footballer whose talent has redefined his role, creating in the process something new and excitingly disruptive. He is an extraordinary player in so many ways, a full-back who operates at a constant level of creative urgency."

PUNDIT:

DANNY MURPHY, BBC MATCH OF THE DAY
"It was a dominant, intelligent, impressive display from the whole team, although Leicester did help them. They tweaked their system and played James Maddison off the left. He normally plays as a 10 and gravitated towards the centre of the pitch, which left Trent Alexander-Arnold to have the freedom of the King Power Stadium."

LEICESTER CITY (4-1-4-1): Schmeichel (C), Ricardo, Evans, Söyüncü, Chilwell, Ndidi, Barnes (Albrighton 58), Praet (Perez 72), Tielemans, Maddison (Choudhury 76), Vardy. Subs not used: Ward, Justin, Morgan, Gray. Booked: Maddison.

LIVERPOOL (4-3-3): Alisson, Alexander-Arnold, Gomez, van Dijk, Robertson, Keita (Milner 70), Henderson (C) (Lallana 82), Wijnaldum, Salah (Origi 70), Firmino, Mane. Subs not used: Adrian, Shaqiri, Jones, Williams. Booked: Gomez.

MANAGER: JÜRGEN KLOPP
"It was exactly the performance we needed. We had no real problems in the game because the boys were really 100% in the game and that helped us a lot. We were very concentrated and the goals were absolutely nice. An important day for us."

FOR THE RECORD:
Roberto Firmino's second goal was the 500th scored by Liverpool under Jürgen Klopp with each of the Brazilian's last nine coming away from Anfield.

ALSO THIS WEEKEND:
• Wolverhampton Wanderers 3-2 Manchester City
• Chelsea 0-2 Southampton
• Manchester United 4-1 Newcastle United

REPORT:

Amazon Prime is usually associated with Boxing Day sales rather than Boxing Day games, but having acquired Premier League TV rights for the round of festive fixtures they selected an 8pm kick-off for Liverpool's trip to Leicester City.

You're more likely to see Santa on his sleigh ride home to the North Pole than public transport at that time on a Boxing Day night, so Liverpool FC offered free coach travel for travelling Kopites to get to the King Power Stadium in exchange for a £5 donation to the North Liverpool Foodbank.

As late a finish as it was, they'll have enjoyed the journey home as Liverpool thrashed the Foxes 4-0 – the widest margin of victory in a game between the top two in the Premier League for eight years.

What's more, they did so without allowing Leicester a single shot on target, an achievement that shouldn't be underestimated considering Brendan Rodgers' side had netted in each of their previous 16 games, racking up 42 goals in the process.

Only the Reds and Manchester City had beaten Leicester during that time and, with Liverpool having spent the week before Christmas becoming World Champions in Qatar, there was an argument to say this could be their toughest game of the season so far. It proved to be a night when the Reds rubber-stamped their status as champions elect.

Sadio Mane could've scored within a minute, but touched the ball wide from Mo Salah's cross, before the Egyptian struck the side-netting from a wide angle after zipping past Kasper Schmeichel to reach Naby Keita's through-ball first.

The breakthrough came in the 31st minute when Trent Alexander-

Arnold crossed to the far post for Roberto Firmino to head home. Only the outstretched arm of Schmeichel prevented Mane from making it two in two minutes after a mistake by Jonny Evans.

Leicester had nothing in response and the second half turned into something of a virtuoso performance from Alexander-Arnold, who ran the game from right-back. How many other players can do that?

It was from his corner that Caglar Söyüncü handled the ball. Michael Oliver pointed to the spot, VAR backed him up and James Milner, who'd only been on the pitch for a minute, stepped up to convert a 71st minute penalty, sending Schmeichel the wrong way.

Three minutes later Alexander-Arnold was the creator again. This time he received a pass from Milner on the right and flashed a low cross to Firmino, who controlled the ball with the outstep of his right

boot before curling it into the top corner with his instep. Making the difficult look easy is part of Firmino's skill-set, and also Alexander-Arnold's.

Liverpool's fourth, coming in the 78th minute, was breathtaking. Gini Wijnaldum set Mane charging through the middle and he slipped the ball to his right, where the rampaging Alexander-Arnold met it with an unerring first-time finish. He celebrated with his arms folded, ala Kylian Mbappe, in front of the travelling Kop as they went wild in the visitors' corner of the King Power Stadium.

It was noted in Paris – "Yeah, I saw! I'm proud. This guy is amazing," Mbappe later said, but this was a night when everyone took note of Jürgen Klopp's Liverpool as they extended the advantage over their closest challengers to 13 points in the most emphatic way possible.

REPORT:

Liverpool began the decade at Anfield with a 2-1 FA Cup 3rd round replay defeat to Championship side Reading. They ended it with a 1-0 Premier League victory against Wolves to make it 50 home league games unbeaten and remain 13 points clear at the top of the table.

And, if any further evidence was needed to display how times have changed for the Reds over the last 10 years, the major talking point from this tough, often disjointed, clash was the role of VAR in deciding the outcome.

There was a new addition to Liverpool's deep-red jerseys as they entered the field of play. Winning the FIFA Club World Cup final against Flamengo in Qatar earned Jürgen Klopp's team the right to wear the gold FIFA Champions Badge on their shirts, the Premier League giving the Reds permission to do so against Wolves as a one-off.

So new gold met the men in old gold and it was the world champions that started better. When Sadio Mane freed Trent Alexander-Arnold on the right to cross low to the front post in the fourth minute, it looked like the Anfield Road end net would soon be bulging, but Mo Salah's deft flick guided the ball narrowly over the crossbar.

Wolves, well-organised by Nuno Espirito Santo, then prevented the Reds from forging any real clear-cut opportunities until the game exploded into life in the final three minutes of the half. Virgil van Dijk's pass was chested down by Adam Lallana to Mane, who side-footed the ball past Rui Patricio. 1-0, but referee Anthony Taylor cut the celebrations short, ruling the ball had hit Lallana's arm.

VAR intervened and, just as it had appeared with the naked eye, concluded that Lallana hadn't handled it. The goal was given. One nil to Liverpool, leaving the Wolves players with a burning sense of injustice that was inflamed moments later.

Jonny crossed from the Liverpool left to Pedro Neto, who smashed the ball past Alisson before running the width of the pitch to slide on his knees in front of the team benches, cupping his hands to his ears. His unbridled joy was soon extinguished when VAR ruled that Jonny's foot had been offside before he crossed the ball.

It was a marginal decision that went in Liverpool's favour but, having previously had goals disallowed against Aston Villa and Watford for offside armpits, if you lose out to a black and white rule then you get to gain from it too.

Perhaps a little bit of fatigue finally caught up with the Reds as the two best opportunities of the second half fell to Wolves, but Alisson palmed Diogo Jota's effort wide before Joe Gomez, who was outstanding at centre-half, made a fine block to divert a Raul Jimenez attempt over.

That was enough to add another win, another clean sheet and another three points to a tally of 55 – the highest total Liverpool have ended any decade with.

LIVERPOOL 1
WOLVERHAMPTON WANDERERS 0
Goal: Mane (42)

29.12.19 • Anfield • Attendance: 53,326
Referee: Anthony Taylor

LIVERPOOL (4-2-3-1): Alisson, Alexander-Arnold, Gomez, van Dijk, Robertson, Henderson (C), Wijnaldum (Milner 86), Lallana (Keita 67), Firmino (Origi 86), Mane, Salah. Subs not used: Adrian, Jones, Elliott, Williams. Booked: Lallana.

WOLVERHAMPTON WANDERERS (4-5-1): Patricio, Bennett, Coady (C), Kilman, Jonny, Dendoncker (Traore 58), Neves (Saiss 58), Moutinho, Vinagre, Neto, Jota (Jimenez 72). Subs not used: Ruddy, Doherty, Otasowie, Buur. Booked: Espirito Santo.

PRESS BOX:

CHRIS WHEELER, DAILY MAIL

"Liverpool's winning goal by Sadio Mane in the 42nd minute was allowed to stand following a two-minute review, after Anthony Taylor had initially disallowed it for handball by Adam Lallana. It was the correct decision as Lallana controlled Virgil van Dijk's pass with his shoulder."

PUNDIT:

GRAEME SOUNESS, SKY SPORTS

"We should change it [the offside rule] to: if any part of the striker is onside. So his foot could be behind the line, but if most of his body is beyond it, we should allow the goal to stand. It would take away the majority of the grey areas and we'd see more goals."

MANAGER: JÜRGEN KLOPP

"It was a tough test and rightly so. First half we were good and controlled the game, but I can imagine Wolves were not happy with the VAR decisions. However, the momentum went with them after that moment."

FOR THE RECORD:

This was Liverpool's 50th league game unbeaten at Anfield. It's only the third time a team has gone unbeaten in the top-flight for 50 games or more.

ALSO THIS WEEKEND:

• Arsenal 1-2 Chelsea
• Manchester City 2-0 Sheffield United
• Norwich City 2-2 Tottenham Hotspur

LIVERPOOL 2
SHEFFIELD UNITED 0

Goals: Salah (4), Mane (64)
02.01.20 • Anfield • Attendance: 53,321
Referee: Paul Tierney

LIVERPOOL (4-3-3): Alisson, Alexander-Arnold, Gomez, van Dijk, Robertson (Lallana 88), Milner, J Henderson (C), Wijnaldum, Salah (Elliott 90), Firmino, Mane (Origi 78). Subs not used: Adrian, Phillips, Jones, Williams.

SHEFFIELD UNITED (3-5-2): D Henderson, Basham, Egan, O'Connell, Baldock, Lundstram, Norwood (C) (Besic 78), Fleck, Stevens, McGoldrick (Sharp 66), Mousset (McBurnie 65). Subs not used: Verrips, Robinson, Jagielka, Osborn.

PRESS BOX:
LEON WOBSCHALL, YORKSHIRE EVENING POST
"A dazzling interchange between Salah and Mane ended in the latter seeing his toe-poke blocked by Henderson, with the Senegalese striker tucking away the rebound. It was the moment of quality that Liverpool were always likely to unleash from their locker at some juncture and effectively sealed the game as a competitive entity."

PUNDIT:
RIO FERDINAND, BT SPORT
"James Milner is the only one who has won a Premier League title in that dressing-room so a lot will be looking at him, but a lot of them will using the manager as that yard stick, and saying we don't want to get carried away."

REPORT:

Rarely do you hear a Premier League manager full of detailed praise, in his post-match interview, for an opponent his team has just lost to.

So, after goals from Mo Salah and Sadio Mane kicked Liverpool's 2020 off with a 2-0 win against Sheffield United at Anfield, it was refreshing to hear Blades' boss Chris Wilder give a straight-talking assessment of Jürgen Klopp's side.

"They won every first ball, every second ball, dropped on every second ball, ran forward and ran back and they did that miles better than us. So when academy coaches and all this nonsense that comes out about coaching, have a little peek at Liverpool tonight.

"They played in second and third gear but still had the humility and desire to do that as world champions, European champions and,

obviously, they're well on the way to being Premier League champions.

"You just look at the appetite and the desire of everybody around the football club, it's got a feeling of a relentlessness about them and the supporters as well, the way they drive their players on. They realise what a huge, important season it is and a fantastic position they're in.

"Thankfully we've played Liverpool twice! I wish Jürgen and Liverpool all the best. I love everything about them, the way they go about tactical and technical players. But the top bit, the physical and mental part of it, is amazing, and if that's good enough for them it's certainly good enough for anybody else."

The details of how the match was won almost seem incidental when you hear Wilder speaking so effusively about a Liverpool team that made it 18 consecutive league wins at Anfield and have gone

58

W

MANAGER: JÜRGEN KLOPP

"We controlled the game. We played around their formation, played behind, in-between, broke the lines and had counter-attacks. All the things we want to have. The boys played sensational. The way we controlled Sheffield United was exceptional."

FOR THE RECORD:

Alisson's clean sheet was his fifth in a row in the Premier League, the best run by a Liverpool goalkeeper since Pepe Reina in September 2007.

ALSO THIS MIDWEEK:

• Manchester City 2-1 Everton
• Arsenal 2-0 Manchester United
• Newcastle United 0-3 Leicester City

unbeaten in the top-flight for a full calendar year.

Salah had the ball in the net after just four minutes when Virgil van Dijk's arrowed pass allowed Andy Robertson to get in behind George Baldock, who slipped as he chased back. Robertson crossed low, Salah raced in at the near post to convert. 1-0.

The Reds' no.11 almost made it two when he clipped Jordan Henderson's cross towards the top corner, only for Blades keeper Dean Henderson to produce an outstanding save to flick the ball over.

After keeping out Salah again before the interval, goalkeeper Henderson could only watch as the Egyptian forward's chipped cross beat everyone only to rebound back off the inside of his post. Then Salah turned provider.

Mane sprinted down the left and exchanged passes with Salah before stretching to shoot goalwards. The advancing Henderson took the pace off his shot, but the ball continued to roll goalwards before Mane helped it over the line.

Sheffield United had a gilt-edged chance to pull a late goal back when Oli McBurnie slid in at the far post to meet boyhood Liverpool fan Jack O'Connell's pass, but he only managed to knock the ball down into the turf before Alisson grabbed it to complete another Reds' victory that even Chris Wilder appreciated.

TOTTENHAM HOTSPUR 0
LIVERPOOL 1

Goal: Firmino (37)

11.01.20 • Tottenham Hotspur Stadium •
Attendance: 61,023
Referee: Martin Atkinson

PRESS BOX:

JOHN CROSS, DAILY MIRROR

"It has taken time to get to this point, but from the first game Klopp's demands on his players were obvious and they have never stopped. Spurs boss Jose Mourinho even admitted his players would 'collapse' if they tried to match Liverpool's intensity. It is impossible to think of a team which comes close to Liverpool's fitness levels."

PUNDIT:

TONY CASCARINO, THE TIMES

"The way Firmino let the ball run across him in order to make space for himself was genius. He always knows what is around him, all over the pitch. He is a thinking player who always seems to know what is the best option to take. He makes Liverpool tick."

TOTTENHAM HOTSPUR (4-5-1): Gazzaniga, Tanganga, Alderweireld (C), Sanchez, Rose (Lamela 69), Aurier, Eriksen (Lo Celso 69), Moura, Alli, Winks, Son. Subs not used: Vorm, Vertonghen, Dier, Sessegnon, Skipp.

LIVERPOOL (4-3-3): Alisson, Alexander-Arnold, Gomez, van Dijk, Robertson, Oxlade-Chamberlain (Lallana 61), Henderson (C), Wijnaldum, Salah (Shaqiri 90), Firmino, Mane (Origi 81). Subs not used: Adrian, Minamino, Phillips, Williams.
Booked: Gomez, Oxlade-Chamberlain.

TOTTENHAM HOTSPUR v LIVERPOOL

MANAGER: JÜRGEN KLOPP

"The result is the most important thing. There was one team who deserved to win and that was us. That the game was not decided after 50 or 60 minutes was our fault as well. We should have scored more goals, that's the truth."

FOR THE RECORD:

This was Liverpool's 38th Premier League game without the defeat, in which time they've accumulated 104 points – a PL record over a 38-game period.

ALSO THIS WEEKEND:

• Leicester City 1-2 Southampton
• Aston Villa 1-6 Manchester City
• Bournemouth 0-3 Watford

REPORT:

Liverpool's first win at a new ground, the magnificent 62,303-capacity Tottenham Hotspur Stadium, to make it 56 different away venues that the Reds have emerged victorious at, would normally be the Premier League record that caught the eye after this 1-0 win.

Not today. Not when we're talking about this Liverpool team. Not when we're talking about reaching unprecedented territory on a European scale.

Victory took the Redmen to 61 points from their opening 21 games, the first time in the history of any of the big five European leagues that a club has made such a good start to a season. It was also Liverpool's 38th consecutive league game unbeaten – not just another club record, but the equivalent of an entire season undefeated.

The Reds dominated possession, but breaking down Tottenham's white wall proved tricky. Roberto Firmino's early shot was blocked by debutant right-back Japhet Tanganga, and when Alex Oxlade-Chamberlain fired in the rebound it looked a goal all the way until the base of the post sent the ball bouncing back out against Tanganga, before falling kindly for Paulo Gazzaniga to collect.

Virgil van Dijk was denied next with his 22nd minute header, from Jordan Henderson's cross, destined for the net until Gazzaniga saved brilliantly, but the Tottenham keeper couldn't stop Firmino a quarter-of-an-hour later. Henderson bravely headed the ball forward on the edge of the penalty area to Mo Salah, who slipped a pass towards Firmino.

Tanganga expected the Brazilian to strike the ball with his right foot, but Firmino allowed it to run across his body onto his left, taking the young Spurs defender out of the equation. He then took one sublime touch before firing the ball home and celebrating by placing a hand over his left eye, a reference to the eye injury he suffered when Liverpool beat Spurs at Wembley in 2018. It was also clear to see it was a world class goal that ultimately settled the game.

Salah should really have added a second after dispossessing Davidson Sanchez only to shoot wide, while after the break Trent Alexander-Arnold dragged a shot past the post and Gazzaniga saved Mane's header. Then Tottenham got the late chances they'd waited all game for.

Lucas Moura teed up Heung-Min Son, but he fired over, and quite how substitute Giovani Lo Celso turned Serge Aurier's wicked late cross wide of Alisson's far post only he will know. It certainly shocked Jose Mourinho, who collapsed to his knees with his arms held aloft.

With Alisson producing a textbook display of handling to keep a sixth consecutive clean sheet – Liverpool's best run since December 2006 – the Reds held onto their 1-0 lead to secure three vital points from a game that only one side was trying to win.

Setting an unprecedented new European record in the process was a bonus, but you don't need to look at the record books to understand the standard the European and World Champions are setting.

The Premier League table says it all.

LIVERPOOL v MANCHESTER UNITED

W

LIVERPOOL 2
MANCHESTER UNITED 0
Goals: Van Dijk (14), Salah (90)
19.01.20 • Anfield • Attendance: 52,916
Referee: Craig Pawson

LIVERPOOL (4-3-3): Alisson, Alexander-Arnold, Gomez, van Dijk, Robertson, Oxlade-Chamberlain (Lallana 65), Henderson (C), Wijnaldum, Salah, Firmino (Origi 82), Mane (Fabinho 82). Subs not used: Adrian, Minamino, Matip, Jones.
Booked: Salah.

MANCHESTER UNITED (3-5-2): de Gea, Linderlof, Maguire (C), Shaw (Dalot 87), Wan-Bissaka, Fred, Matic, Pereira (Mata 74), Williams (Greenwood 74), James, Martial. Subs not used: Romero, Bailly, Jones, Lingard.
Booked: Matic, de Gea, Shaw.

PRESS BOX:
HENRY WINTER, THE TIMES
"From Trent Alexander-Arnold's corner, Harry Maguire was blocked off by Joe Gomez and van Dijk made his move. Chased by Brandon Williams, van Dijk steamed imperiously through United's defence like a majestic liner arriving up the Mersey, cheered on by crowds of onlookers."

PUNDIT:
JAMIE CARRAGHER, SKY SPORTS
"Everyone in the country is going to think that's the Premier League won. This is a phenomenal team. They are the best in the league, the best in Europe and the best in the world at the moment."

MANAGER: JÜRGEN KLOPP
"Of course they are allowed to dream, free to sing whatever they want, as long as they do their job when we play. We will not be part of that party yet, but it's no problem. At the moment, even in the living rooms in front of the televisions, there is a lot of passion around the world based on Liverpool Football Club and we can take energy from that."

FOR THE RECORD:
Virgil van Dijk's goal meant Liverpool had scored in each of their opening 22 league games of the season for the first time in the club's history.

ALSO THIS WEEKEND:
• Manchester City 2-2 Crystal Palace
• Burnley 2-1 Leicester City
• Newcastle 1-0 Chelsea

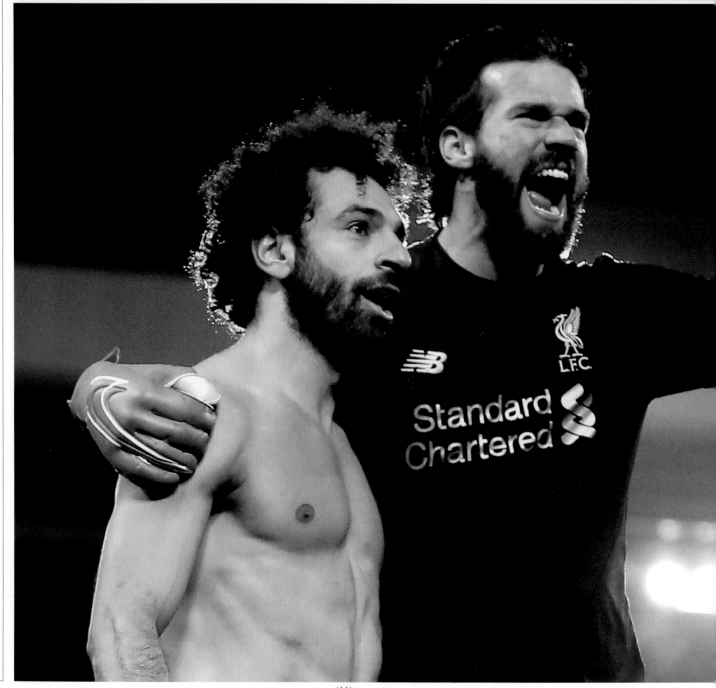

REPORT:

When you've not won the league for 30 years the last thing you want to do is count your chickens before they've hatched, but sometimes a moment comes along when an outpouring of pure, unbridled joy is impossible to contain. That moment came at Anfield against Manchester United.

Liverpool should have been out of sight by the time the game went into stoppage time, but with only Virgil van Dijk's header separating the two great rivals there was a sense of nervous tension in the cold night air.

When Aaron Wan-Bissaka weakly mishit a stoppage-time shot at Alisson most goalkeepers would have collapsed onto the ball to waste a few seconds, but Alisson is not most goalkeepers. Spotting Mo Salah completely unmarked on the half-way line, he ignored his team-mates, who were pleading with him to keep hold of the ball, and launched a perfect pass to send the Egyptian scampering through on goal.

Daniel James, the visitors' quickest player, chased Salah down, but by the time he could make a challenge the Liverpool striker was in the Kop penalty area slotting a low shot between David de Gea's legs to make it Liverpool 2 Manchester United 0. The roar that greeted the goal was of a decibel level not heard all season.

Loud doesn't do it justice, and the sight of Alisson running the full length of the pitch to celebrate with a shirtless Salah in front of the Kop – a la Pepe Reina after David Ngog's goal against the Red Devils in 2009 – made it feel all the more iconic, all the more historic.

The explosion of noise was a collective release of both joy and relief, a moment when Liverpool supporters, with their team 16 points clear at the top of the table with a game in hand, let the lid come off their previously contained excitement.

"We're gonna win the league, we're gonna win the league. And now yer gonna believe us, and now yer gonna believe us, and NOW yer gonna believe us...we're gonna win the league."

Having not been sung all season, despite a record-breaking start that means the Reds had taken 91 points out of the last 93 available, 64 of them this season, it was significant that United were the opponents when this inevitable chant finally emerged.

After three decades of being taunted by Manchester United supporters about Liverpool's failure to win the Premier League, this was the moment when Kopites pointed out that the wait is nearly over.

Ole Gunnar Solskjaer's side were fortunate to still be in the game at that point. After van Dijk's thumping 14th minute header, from a Trent Alexander-Arnold corner, had broken the deadlock, Liverpool dominated with only VAR, an assistant referee and de Gea denying them further goals.

Roberto Firmino curled home a second, but amidst ferocious Manchester United protests that saw de Gea booked for complaining that he'd been fouled by van Dijk, VAR intervened and chalked the goal off. That Sky Sports' Gary Neville and Roy Keane both thought there was no foul and it should have stood says it all.

With the Reds playing some scintillating football, Gini Wijnaldum had the ball in the net again only for a borderline offside call to correctly deny him, while de Gea did well to stop a Sadio Mane effort with his right foot when the Senegalese striker raced through.

Liverpool came out flying after the break, but with Salah and Mane both putting chances wide, and de Gea pulling off a magnificent save to tip a powerful Jordan Henderson effort onto the post, United remained in the game and had their chance to equalise when Anthony Martial got free in the box, but wildly lashed his effort over.

That was as close as Manchester United got all day and when Salah secured the victory, sending the Reds a whopping 30 points clear of the Mancunians having played a game less, it felt like a watershed moment that will forever be remembered in Anfield folklore.

WOLVERHAMPTON WANDERERS 1
LIVERPOOL 2

Goals: Jimenez (51); Henderson (8), Firmino (84)

23.01.20 • Molineux • Attendance: 31,746
Referee: Michael Oliver

WOLVERHAMPTON WANDERERS (3-4-1-2): Patricio, Dendoncker, Coady (C), Saiss, Doherty, Neves, Moutinho (Gibbs-White 87), Jonny, Neto (Jota 77), Traore, Jimenez. Subs not used: Ruddy, Boly, Giles, Kilman, Ashley-Seal.

LIVERPOOL (4-3-3): Alisson, Alexander-Arnold, Gomez, van Dijk, Robertson, Oxlade-Chamberlain (Fabinho 70), Henderson (C), Wijnaldum, Salah (Origi 85), Firmino, Mane (Minamino 33).
Subs not used: Adrian, Matip, Jones, Williams. Booked: Robertson.

PRESS BOX:
PAUL GORST, LIVERPOOL ECHO
"It is an unshakable, irrepressible mindset more than anything else that has put Liverpool on the brink of title glory. It is now 11 games that have been won by a one-goal margin. Somehow, they always end up on the right side of history."

PUNDIT:
PETER CROUCH, BT SPORT
"Liverpool are well on their way to being a great team. I played with some top, top players, but this team is probably better. We had a midfield of Gerrard, Alonso and Mascherano. Liverpool fans sang at the time it was the best midfield in the world, but the ethos, the atmosphere, the intensity this Liverpool team is playing at, as a collective team, is the best I've seen for a long time."

MANAGER: JÜRGEN KLOPP

"We had incredible chances in the first half and then at the end it was a magic moment from Bobby. The boys are human. It was a little bit up and down. You just have to find a way to win and have someone who makes the perfect decision and that was Bobby again."

FOR THE RECORD:

Liverpool became the first club to win three top-flight games on a Thursday in the same season since Leicester City in 1933/34.

ALSO THIS WEEKEND:
• Sheffield United 0-1 Manchester City
• Chelsea 2-2 Arsenal
• Manchester United 0-2 Burnley

REPORT:

Twenty-two victories from 23 league games. 14 wins on the spin. 94 points taken from the last 96 available. Unprecedented stuff, and this 2-1 success at Wolves was one of the hardest-fought wins of the lot.

Just like they had done at Anfield in December, Nuno Espirito Santo's side gave the Reds quite a game. Jürgen Klopp highlighted before kick-off that Wolves' style of play is different to that of any other club in the Premier League, while they are also one of the few teams that stick to their principles, rather than adapt their formation, when playing Liverpool. It made for another absorbing contest.

Trent Alexander-Arnold is the king of assists and his 22nd in the Premier League, since the start of last season, came in the eighth minute when Jordan Henderson headed his out-swinging corner in off the near post. It was a rare headed goal from the captain who caught out his marker, Joao Moutinho, by charging in to meet the ball when he usually remains on the edge of the box.

A little over half-an-hour in, Sadio Mane signalled to the bench that his race was run. A muscle injury forced him off, allowing Takumi Minamino to make his Premier League debut. Within moments, a Minamino flick over the head of Matt Doherty was going viral on Twitter.

The second half was less than 90 seconds old when Mo Salah robbed Adama Traore of possession on the edge of his own box and struck a powerful low shot goalwards, but Rui Patricio dived to his left to push the ball away. After that, Wolves seized control of the game.

Traore created the equaliser in the 51st minute when he blazed away down the Liverpool left to cross for Raul Jimenez to head home. Then, in the space of three minutes, Alisson was forced to make vital saves to deny both Traore and Jimenez – blocking the Mexican striker's shot with his face.

Fabinho's introduction in the 70th minute was a shrewd move by Klopp. All of a sudden, Liverpool were back in control and when Gini Wijnaldum found Roberto Firmino in the box only Patricio's outstretched left foot prevented the Brazilian from netting. He wouldn't be denied in the 84th minute, though.

Salah nutmegged Ruben Neves on the edge of the box and, as the ball ran loose, Henderson threaded it into Firmino's path. After shifting it onto his left foot, he whipped it into the far corner. Get in! It was Firmino's 10th goal of the season, all of them away from Anfield.

There was still time for Traore to create a 92nd minute chance for Diogo Jota, but he leant back and lifted the ball high and wide from just six yards out. Game over.

With a game-in-hand at West Ham still to come, it left the Reds leading the pack by 16 points and extended the club-record unbeaten league run to a whopping 40-games.

At this rate, the unbeatables will soon be uncatchable.

WEST HAM UNITED 0
LIVERPOOL 2

Goals: Salah (35pen), Oxlade-Chamberlain (52)

29.01.20 • London Stadium • **Attendance:** 59,959
Referee: Jon Moss

PRESS BOX:
SAM WALLACE, DAILY TELEGRAPH
"Having now beaten every one of the league's other 19 teams, Klopp's players have the knack of tuning into what it will take to beat any team on any given day. At some point they may well suffer a misjudgment, but they are now nine games from beating Arsenal's 49-game unbeaten run."

PUNDIT:
JIMMY CARTER, BBC RADIO MERSEYSIDE
"It was a great performance once again from Liverpool. There was great determination and character and it was never in doubt. Once Liverpool went in front there wasn't any doubt whatsoever and the fans will travel back up to Merseyside tonight in good spirits."

WEST HAM UNITED (3-5-1-1): Fabianski, Diop, Ogbonna, Cresswell, Ngakia, Snodgrass, Rice, Noble (C), Masuaku, Lanzini (Fornals 69), Haller. Subs not used: Randolph, Balbuena, Zabaleta, Sanchez, Cardoso, Ajeti. Booked: Diop, Noble.

LIVERPOOL (4-3-3): Alisson, Alexander-Arnold (Keita 77), Gomez, van Dijk, Robertson, Oxlade-Chamberlain (Jones 85), Henderson (C), Wijnaldum, Salah, Firmino, Origi (Fabinho 69). Subs not used: Adrian, Lovren, Minamino, Matip.

MANAGER: JÜRGEN KLOPP

"Yes we have 70 points, an incredible number, but so many things can happen. I'm not too much concerned about records. We had a record at [Borussia] Dortmund and Bayern [Munich] beat it the next season. We don't feel as though anything is done, I promise you."

FOR THE RECORD:

Liverpool became the earliest ever team to beat every other side in a top-flight campaign, beating the 1888/89 Preston North End team that achieved the same feat on 9th February 1899 by 11 days.

ALSO THIS MIDWEEK:

• No other Premier League fixtures

REPORT:

Nineteen points clear and all 19 Premier League rivals now beaten for the first time in the same top-flight season. It was a night when it felt like a case of when, not if, Liverpool's 19th league title will be won.

Almost a year earlier, the Reds went to West Ham on a Monday night having played a game less than Manchester City. The opportunity to turn a two-point lead into five points was missed with a 1-1 draw.

This time Jürgen Klopp's side didn't make the same mistake and extended their gigantic, surely unassailable, 16 point lead over Manchester City to 19 points, comfortably winning their game in hand 2-0. It was a 15th consecutive league win and takes the Reds' astonishing run to 97 points from the last 99 available. Yet another unprecedented achievement.

Sadio Mane's injury meant a start for Divock Origi, and it was a foul on the Belgian than led to Liverpool's opening goal in the 35th minute, although not before Andy Robertson had seen his shot scrambled away from the goalmouth.

David Moyes' side had spent the half camped out behind the halfway line, but when Roberto Firmino controlled Trent Alexander-Arnold's pass in the penalty area and turned it back inside to Origi, the Hammers defence were caught out. Jeremy Ngakia nibbled at an ankle, Issa Diop lunged in and brought Origi down.

VAR failed to find good reason to overturn the decision, and up stepped Mo Salah to strike a venomous penalty into the bottom corner, sending Lukasz Fabianski the wrong way.

Liverpool controlled the second half. Firmino's low shot was turned around the post by Fabianski, but it was a matter of time before the Reds struck again and it came from a West Ham corner.

Virgil van Dijk cleared, Jordan Henderson helped the ball on to Salah and, using the outside of his left boot, he sent Alex Oxlade-Chamberlain sprinting through. Manuel Lanzini tried to take him out, but only bounced off the Ox's body before he slotted home his seventh goal of the season.

Fabianski saved again, this time from Origi, before Alisson was finally called into action to palm away a Declan Rice shot, Alexander-Arnold inadvertently volleying the rebound back against his own post.

The woodwork at the other end of the London Stadium was rattling moments later when Salah struck it from the edge of the box, while Alisson again saved from Rice, this time diving to his right to brilliantly push the ball away. It was his eighth clean sheet of the season to put the Brazilian joint-top of the Golden Glove table, a remarkable statistic given he has missed eight of LFC's 24 games.

More significantly, Klopp's 150th win as LFC manager took the relentless Reds to 70 points – more than they have accumulated in 17 of the previous 27 Premier League seasons – and another big step closer to that 19th league title.

LIVERPOOL 4
SOUTHAMPTON 0

Goals: Oxlade-Chamberlain (47),
Henderson (60), Salah (71, 90)

01.02.20 • Anfield • Attendance: 53,291
Referee: Kevin Friend

LIVERPOOL (4-3-3): Alisson, Alexander-Arnold, Gomez, van Dijk, Robertson,
Henderson (C) (Lallana 88), Fabinho, Wijnaldum (Minamino 81), Salah, Firmino,
Oxlade-Chamberlain (Keita 73).
Subs not used: Adrian, Lovren, Origi, Matip.

SOUTHAMPTON (4-3-3): McCarthy, Ward-Prowse, Stephens, Bednarek, Bertrand,
Djenepo (Boufal 82), Romeu, Hojbjerg (C), Redmond, Ings (Adams 70), Long (Obafemi 70).
Subs not used: Gunn, Vestergaard, Smallbone, Danso.
Booked: Ward-Prowse, Stephens.

PRESS BOX:

RICHARD JOLLY, THE INDEPENDENT

"Seeing off Southampton brought a 16th straight
Premier League victory and sent Liverpool 22 points
clear. They have 20 straight home league wins,
equalling Manchester City's [Premier League] record.
Most remarkably, they have 100 points from a possible
102."

PUNDIT:

JASON McATEER, LFCTV

"You can see why Southampton have taken points
away from home. They created 17 chances and tested
Alisson, but once Liverpool got their first one – and
certainly the second one – they resigned themselves to
it being an uphill battle and Liverpool ended up running
out comfortable winners."

REPORT:

After watching Roberto Firmino create three of Liverpool's four
second half goals against Southampton to go 22 points clear at the
top of the Premier League, Jürgen Klopp compared the Brazilian to
a postman.

"Even Bobby needs an address where he can send the ball," he said.
"How he uses the skill of his mates is special. I do not know a player
like him."

Perhaps the Liverpool manager needs to rethink his analogy – the
postman always rings twice whereas Firmino knocked three passes
to team-mates to score – but there was no doubting he was the star
of a second half show that added even more statistical triumphs to a
scarcely believable run of form.

A 20th consecutive home league win leaves the Reds one behind

the club – and English – record of 21, set between January 1972
and January 1973. A 42nd consecutive top-flight game undefeated
equalled the second ever longest run, set by Brian Clough's
Nottingham Forest in 1978. And from the last 102 points available to
win, Liverpool have now taken 100.

Astonishing stuff. Yet all of those records looked in doubt during
a first half when Southampton, playing with an attack-minded 4-3-3
formation featuring ex-Red Danny Ings, had 10 shots on goal – the
most in the first half by a team visiting Anfield since Klopp has been
LFC manager.

Ings, Shane Long and Moussa Djenepo all went close – as did
Virgil van Dijk with a cheeky back-heel at the other end – but Long
also almost presented Liverpool with a penalty when he dragged

MANAGER: JÜRGEN KLOPP

"We're not even close to being perfect. We just look to use our skills in the best possible way. The boys have done that for a while pretty good and that's why we have these numbers. We didn't want a 22-point lead. We wanted 73 points at the end of today."

FOR THE RECORD:

Liverpool kept their 100th clean sheet under Jürgen Klopp's management in what was his 248th game in charge.

ALSO THIS WEEKEND:
- Tottenham 2-0 Manchester City
- Leicester City 2-2 Chelsea
- Manchester United 0-0 Wolverhampton Wanderers

Firmino to the turf on the goalline only for VAR to turn a blind eye to the offence.

Southampton boss Ralph Hasenhüttl felt similarly aggrieved early in the second half when VAR decided Ings hadn't been tripped by Fabinho in the box, and that passage of play ended with Firmino sublimely flicking the ball to Alex Oxlade-Chamberlain, who rifled home the opening goal.

An end-to-end Liverpool move then saw Firmino play Salah in to score, only for the assistant referee's flag to intervene, but just moments later Firmino pulled the ball back to Jordan Henderson and the Liverpool skipper gloriously side-footed it into the roof of the net.

It was now a case of Saints v Winners and when Henderson's inch-perfect pass sent Salah scurrying clear again the Egyptian waited for

Alex McCarthy to go to ground before dinking the ball over him to make it 3-0.

McCarthy prevented Firmino from getting on the scoresheet and substitutes Takumi Minamino and Naby Keita got in each other's way when a goal looked inevitable from Salah's pass, but on the dot of the 90th minute Firmino mailed another pass to Salah to bag Liverpool's fourth from close range, the ball looping in off the no.11 under a challenge from James Ward-Prowse.

Southampton didn't deserve to lose by four, yet could have lost by six against a Liverpool side that once again delivered three points at Anfield.

NORWICH CITY 0
LIVERPOOL 1

Goal: Mane (78)

15.02.20 • Carrow Road • Attendance: 27,110
Referee: Stuart Attwell

PRESS BOX:
MARK OGDEN, ESPN

"We are now at the stage where the points and numbers really only matter for the history books, because Klopp's team are destined to win the title in record time and this latest victory ensured that Liverpool remain on course to end their 30-year wait to be champions."

PUNDIT:
JAMIE REDKNAPP, DAILY MAIL

"Sadio Mane's reaction to being told he had just scored his 100th goal in the English game said it all. I was in the Sky Sports studio at Carrow Road and Mane, having been told he'd hit a century, said 'Really? Wow! Thank you.' He had not gone into that game thinking about that personal milestone – he wasn't even aware of it!"

NORWICH CITY (4-2-3-1): Krul, Aarons, Zimmermann, Hanley (C), Byram (Lewis 27), Tettey (Drmic 84), McLean, Rupp (Buendia 83), Duda, Cantwell, Pukki. Subs not used: Fahrmann, Godfrey, Vrancic, Hernandez. Booked: Hanley.

LIVERPOOL (4-3-3): Alisson, Alexander-Arnold, Gomez, van Dijk, Robertson, Wijnaldum (Milner 84), Henderson (C), Keita (Fabinho 60), Salah, Firmino, Oxlade-Chamberlain (Mane 60). Subs not used: Adrian, Lovren, Lallana, Origi. Booked: Keita, Mane.

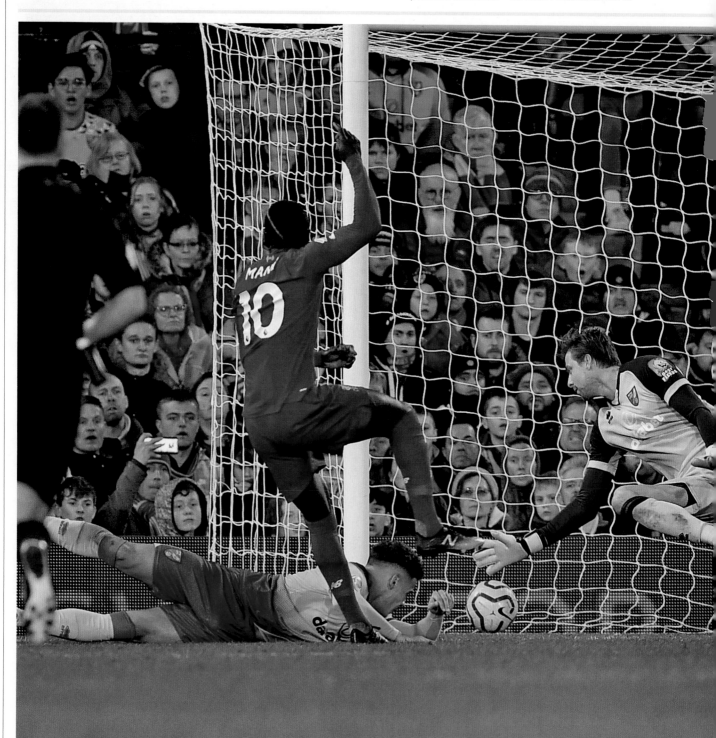

MANAGER: JÜRGEN KLOPP

"The gap is so insane, I don't really understand it. I'm not smart enough. I've not had that before. It's outstanding, it's so difficult. I go back into the changing room and we chat about the things and then I'm like, 'Oh, but congratulations. We won the game, another three points'."

FOR THE RECORD:

Sadio Mane's goal was his 100th in English football and his 75th for Liverpool, but the first he has scored as a substitute for the Reds.

ALSO THIS WEEKEND:
• Wolverhampton Wanderers 0-0 Leicester City
• Southampton 1-2 Burnley
• Arsenal 4-0 Newcastle United

REPORT:

Storm Dennis made it tricky for both teams and bottom-of-the-table Norwich made life difficult for Liverpool, but the Reds again found a way to win to storm 25 points clear at the top of the Premier League.

Sadio Mane, on his return from the muscle injury he suffered at Wolves, proved to be the match-winner after coming on as a 60th minute substitute, but this victory was more about the Reds' perseverance as a team than any individual.

None of the players on show from either team had played for a fortnight due to the Premier League's inaugural winter break. Perhaps it was a factor, perhaps pure co-incidence, but both Liverpool and Norwich looked rusty in an opening 45 minutes that saw very little goalmouth action.

Trent Alexander-Arnold and Naby Keita fired a couple of efforts wide, but it was the Canaries who had the best chance when Lukas Rupp went one-on-one with Alisson, only for the Liverpool goalkeeper to stretch out an arm and paw the ball away like a giant cat when the German opted to pass to Teemu Pukki instead of shooting. It was yet another important save by the Brazilian and even though VAR may have ruled Rupp was offside had Norwich scored, Alisson didn't know that at the time.

There was also a let-off after the break when Alex Tettey rattled the outside of a post with a surprise shot from a wide angle, but other than that the Reds

dominated with the only question being could they find a way past Canaries keeper Tim Krul?

The Dutchman had already palmed a Keita effort over and clutched a Virgil van Dijk header when he made an outstanding double-save in the 59th minute. Mo Salah, as per usual, was surrounded by three players in the box, but somehow created space to fire a right-footed shot goalwards. Krul pushed the ball out into the path of Keita, who seemed certain to score until the Norwich goalkeeper somehow blocked his shot from point-blank range.

A minute later, Klopp introduced Fabinho and Mane from the bench and it proved to be a game-changer. Fabinho's arrival allowed Jordan Henderson to play further forward towards the right, and it was from such a position that the skipper pinged a diagonal pass towards Mane.

The Senegalese international brushed off Christoph Zimmermann, brought the high ball down on his right foot and then swivelled onto his left before burying a low shot past Krul at his near post. It was Mane's 75th goal for the Reds and one of outstanding quality.

With the travelling Kop adding a new song to their repertoire – "hand it over, hand it over, hand it over Manchester" – Roberto Firmino should have added a second, but flashed Alexander-Arnold's cross wide of the target from close range.

Alisson had to hold a late Pukki effort, but his 10th clean sheet in the last 11 games further confirmed that not even Storm Dennis can blow the Reds off course.

LIVERPOOL 3
WEST HAM UNITED 2

Goals: Wijnaldum (9), Salah (68), Mane (81); Diop (12), Fornals (54)

24.02.20 • Anfield • Attendance: 53,313
Referee: Jon Moss

LIVERPOOL (4-3-3): Alisson, Alexander-Arnold, Gomez, van Dijk (C), Robertson, Keita (Oxlade-Chamberlain 57), Fabinho, Wijnaldum, Salah, Firmino, Mane (Matip 90). Subs not used: Adrian, Lovren, Minamino, Lallana, Origi.

WEST HAM UNITED (4-2-3-1): Fabianski, Ngakia, Diop, Ogbonna, Cresswell, Rice, Soucek (Fornals 47), Snodgrass (Bowen 84), Noble (C), Anderson (Haller 65), Antonio. Subs not used: Randolph, Balbuena, Zabaleta, Lanzini. Booked: Rice, Diop, Noble.

PRESS BOX:
JASON BURT, DAILY TELEGRAPH
"The roar around Anfield at the end, with the injured captain Jordan Henderson seeking out goalkeeper Alisson for a bear-hug, said it all as Liverpool collected another win in their inevitable march towards the Premier League title."

PUNDIT:
JAMIE CARRAGHER, SKY SPORTS
"Mo Salah gets a lot of assists too. Only Lionel Messi has more goals and assists than Salah in Europe's top five leagues since he joined Liverpool. The big thing I like about him is that he is never injured. You see Liverpool play and he is there week in and week out."

REPORT:

Trophies, rather than records, has always been the benchmark that Liverpool Football Club judges itself by. Yet history tends to show that when a team enjoys a period of success, records are racked up along the way. Against West Ham United, Jürgen Klopp's class of 2019/20 equalled two biggies.

This 3-2 victory made it 18 consecutive top-flight wins for Liverpool, matching the all-time record set by Manchester City in 2017. It was also the Reds' 21st consecutive top-flight win at home, equalling the all-time record set by Bill Shankly's Liverpool in 1972.

The Premier League trophy being lifted will be the symbolic climax to this incredible league campaign, but such remarkable consistency is the reason why Klopp's men are just four games short of being champions in February. And it felt like February.

The wind was so blustery that one set of steps leading up to the Main Stand had to be closed for safety reasons and, with just 12 minutes on the clock, both teams had scored from headers.

Gini Wijnaldum got the first, stooping to meet a brilliant Trent Alexander-Arnold cross and head past Lukasz Fabianski, who could only help the ball into the net. The Hammers levelled just three minutes later, Issa Diop heading a corner in at the near post to become the first player to net a first-half league goal against Liverpool since Everton's Richarlison on 4th December.

It gave David Moyes' side a foothold in the game, although their goal lead a charmed life with Virgil van Dijk's header hitting the crossbar and Alexander-Arnold seeing two efforts, one from a free-kick, go narrowly wide before half-time.

W

MANAGER: JÜRGEN KLOPP

"I never thought it [Man City's record] would be broken or equalled. We did it and I cannot believe it happened to be honest. When we equalised the stadium was rocking and that helps us. Whatever will happen this season is an effort of all of us. I could not be more thankful or appreciate the support we get."

FOR THE RECORD:

This victory took Liverpool to 79 points, the total number of points the Reds accumulated when last winning the league in 1989/90.

ALSO THIS WEEKEND:

• Leicester City 0-1 Manchester City
• Arsenal 3-2 Everton
• Chelsea 2-1 Tottenham Hotspur

Roberto Firmino lifted an early second half opportunity over the crossbar before West Ham took a shock 54th minute lead when substitute Pablo Fornals clipped Declan Rice's cross past Alisson. Liverpool needed to respond and did so promptly with Klopp introducing Alex Oxlade-Chamberlain from the bench and the Anfield atmosphere ratcheting up a notch or two.

All of a sudden, the West Ham goal was under siege. Oxlade-Chamberlain fired a long-range shot wide, Fabianski saved from van Dijk and Alexander-Arnold, and Firmino headed over as the Reds forced a succession of corners.

An equaliser had to come and it arrived in the 68th minute when Mo Salah connected with Andy Robertson's cross. It wasn't his best strike, but the ball squirmed through the gloves and legs of Fabianski. 2-2.

Anfield was now baying for a winner with every West Ham touch prompting incessant whistles. Firmino almost obliged, his close-range header hitting the post after Fabianski denied Alexander-Arnold, before the Reds' right-back created the winning goal.

He was quickest to react when a Joe Gomez shot was deflected and lifted the ball over Fabianski for Mane to net at the far post. Liverpool's comeback was complete.

Mane had another goal ruled out by VAR, and Alisson had to make a late save from Jarrod Bowen, but yet again the relentless, record-equalling Reds got the job done.

WATFORD 3
LIVERPOOL 0

Goals: Sarr (54, 60), Deeney (72)
29.02.20 • Vicarage Road
Attendance: 21,634
Referee: Michael Oliver

WATFORD (4-2-3-1): Foster, Femenia, Kabasele, Cathcart, Masina, Hughes, Capoue, Sarr (Pussetto 82), Doucoure (Chalobah 89), Deulofeu (Pereyra 37), Deeney (C). Subs not used: Gomes, Dawson, Welbeck, Gray.

LIVERPOOL (4-3-3): Alisson, Alexander-Arnold, Lovren, van Dijk (C), Robertson, Oxlade-Chamberlain (Origi 65), Fabinho, Wijnaldum (Lallana 61), Salah, Firmino (Minamino 79), Mane. Subs not used: Adrian, Matip, Jones, Hoever.

PRESS BOX:

JOE RIMMER, LIVERPOOL ECHO

"There's one thing Klopp will not do when his players gather to sift through the wreckage of Watford. He won't single anyone out. It's what makes Klopp a special manager. Liverpool's success is down to the collective and behind closed doors that approach will ensure the loss does not linger."

PUNDIT:

GILBERTO SILVA, THE TIMES

"Liverpool came very close to the unbeaten record we hold with Arsenal. Even though they did not break it, what Liverpool have done this season is very special. It is not so easy with the competitors these days. Jürgen Klopp, his staff and players have done a good job. They can still do marvellous things."

REPORT:

Nothing lasts forever. Liverpool were always going to lose a Premier League game one day and so it came at Vicarage Road with Watford running out deserved 3-0 winners.

Perhaps the nature of the defeat – by three goals to a club in the relegation zone – was a surprise to some, but anyone who saw how well Nigel Pearson's side played at Anfield in December knew they were a far better team than the league table suggested. History also shows that defeats of this nature in title-winning seasons for LFC are not a new phenomenon.

In 1978/79, when the Reds conceded just 16 goals in 42 games, Bob Paisley's team shipped three in a 3-1 defeat to mid-table Aston Villa at Villa Park. In 1983/84, en-route to winning the league, European Cup and League Cup, Joe Fagan's Reds were beaten 4-0

by Coventry City at Highfield Road. And in 1989/90, the last time that Liverpool emerged as champions, Kenny Dalglish's Reds suffered a 4-1 reverse against Southampton at The Dell.

Such defeats are a reminder of the level top-flight football is at. Have an off-day, as Jürgen Klopp's men undoubtedly did at Vicarage Road, and you get punished. Which only goes to show how truly remarkable it was that Liverpool went 44 Premier League games unbeaten and travelled to Watford on the back of 18 consecutive league wins.

Some critics had suggested those types of numbers indicated that the standard of opposition in the Premier League was poor. Yet for Liverpool to lose 3-0 to 19th-placed Watford, in the same season that defending champions Manchester City lost 3-2 at now 20th-placed

MANAGER: JÜRGEN KLOPP

"We never estimated the situation wrongly, we never thought it would be easy. These boys are working extremely hard. If you win, you do it in the right manner. If you lose, you take it like a man. From time to time, if you are not good enough, you need to restart."

FOR THE RECORD:
Liverpool have now played eight times on 29th February during leap years but have only won on three occasions, the most recent being in 1956 against Leeds United.

ALSO THIS WEEKEND:
• Norwich City 1-0 Leicester City
• Tottenham Hotspur 2-3 Wolverhampton Wanderers
• Everton 1-1 Manchester United

Norwich City, suggests exactly the opposite. How many other top European leagues are so competitive that the bottom two can beat the top two?

Liverpool's sloppy passing was the main issue in the first half with the Reds mustering just one shot on goal, Mo Salah hitting the side netting, while Alisson produced a fine save from Troy Deeney to keep the sides level at the interval.

Strangely, it was two throw-ins that caught Liverpool out in the second half and lead to Ismaila Sarr scoring twice in six minutes. The first, on Liverpool's right, allowed Abdoulaye Doucoure to cross from the byline for Sarr to poke home. And the second, on Liverpool's left, resulted in Sarr running clean through from Will Hughes' pass to lift the ball over Alisson.

A little pat on the back from Sarr's Senegalese international team-mate Sadio Mane, when he returned to the half-way line for the restart, was a lovely sporting gesture on a special day for the 22-year-old.

The Reds tried to respond. Andy Robertson forced Ben Foster to save at his near post and substitute Adam Lallana was unlucky when his shot from the outside of the box struck the upright, but Liverpool's run of scoring in 36 consecutive Premier League matches also came to an end. Hornets skipper Deeney made it 3-0 and with that, Liverpool were finally beaten in their 28th game of the season.

LIVERPOOL v BOURNEMOUTH

W

LIVERPOOL 2
BOURNEMOUTH 1

Goals: Salah (24), Mane (33); C Wilson (9)
07.03.20 • Anfield • Attendance: 53,323
Referee: Paul Tierney

LIVERPOOL (4-3-3): Adrian, Alexander-Arnold, Gomez, van Dijk, Milner (C), Oxlade-Chamberlain (Lallana 84), Fabinho, Wijnaldum, Salah, Firmino (Origi 90), Mane. Subs not used: Lonergan, Keita, Minamino, Matip, Williams.

BOURNEMOUTH (4-5-1): Ramsdale, Stacey, S Cook (C) (Simpson 19), Ake, Smith, Fraser, L Cook, Lerma (Gosling 80), Billing, Stanislas (Solanke 68), C Wilson. Subs not used: Boruc, Surman, Surridge, Rico. Booked: C Wilson.

PRESS BOX:
ANDY HUNTER, THE GUARDIAN
"There was uproar as Wilson escaped with a shove on Joe Gomez in the build-up. It was accompanied by the sound of 50,000-plus bums squeaking. Wilson clearly knocked Gomez off balance as they pursued a clearance into the Liverpool half. Anfield waited for VAR to chalk off Wilson's goal. Surprisingly the wait was in vain."

PUNDIT:
DANNY MURPHY,
BBC MATCH OF THE DAY
"The opening goal, I have to say I agreed with Jürgen Klopp wholeheartedly. It's a free-kick, but even after the push they have to defend better. It was a sloppy start, but it was a free-kick and I don't know why VAR didn't give the push on Gomez. What's he got to do? Dive? Go over?"

MANAGER: JÜRGEN KLOPP
"The biggest chance in the second half was obviously Fraser's chance. Millie saved our life, that helped massively, I really think we deserved that today. We had moments but didn't finish it off. But the attitude again, the reaction to the different knocks, I liked a lot. Super chances, two wonderful goals. So after the final whistle I was really happy."

FOR THE RECORD:
Mo Salah's goal made him the first Liverpool player to score 20 times in three successive seasons since Michael Owen between 2000/01 and 2002/03.

ALSO THIS WEEKEND:
• Manchester United 2-0 Manchester City
• Chelsea 4-0 Everton
• Leicester City 4-0 Aston Villa

REPORT:
After winning 21 consecutive top-flight games at Anfield between January and December 1972, Liverpool's winning streak came to an end in controversial circumstances.

Bill Shankly's Reds faced champions Derby County at a snow-covered Anfield with Brian Clough's Rams taking a 15th minute lead through Roger Davies. "Definitely offside," stormed Shankly afterwards. "I was right beside it and there's no argument about it."

A TV replay later confirmed Shanks was right – Davies was yards offside – with the Liverpool Echo describing it as "a palpable misjudgement by the linesman," and "a calamitous ruling."

So, when Callum Wilson opened the scoring for Bournemouth nine minutes into this clash after blatantly pushing Joe Gomez during the build-up, it appeared that history might repeat itself.

Klopp's Liverpool had also won 21 consecutive top-flight games at Anfield and now they were behind to a controversial early goal that, to the manager's bemusement, wasn't ruled out by VAR. But whereas a goal

from Liverpool's no.10 – John Toshack – was only enough to earn a 1-1 draw in 1972, an assist and a goal from Liverpool's current no.10 – Sadio Mane – created history in 2020.

Adrian and Aaron Ramsdale both made saves to deny Nathan Ake and Roberto Firmino following Wilson's goal before Bournemouth skipper Steve Cook was forced off injured. It proved to be a turning point.

Just five minutes later Mane robbed his replacement, Jack Simpson, of possession before slipping a pass to Mo Salah. The ball was slightly behind the Egyptian, but he adjusted his body to control it before firing a low shot into the bottom corner.

It was Salah's 70th league goal on his 100th Premier League appearance for the Redmen, the most anyone has netted in a century of games, and edged him past Luis Suarez's total of 69. Only South African striker Berry Nieuwenhuys (74) has netted more in the league for Liverpool having been born outside the UK.

The winner came with 33 minutes on the clock and again it was Liverpool's ability

to win possession and counter-attack that proved decisive. Virgil van Dijk intercepted a stray pass and, before Bournemouth knew it, he'd played Mane clean through. The Senegalese international curled the ball beyond Ramsdale for his 18th goal of the season, prompting his manager to celebrate in animated fashion.

Liverpool ran the second half. Van Dijk had a header saved, Roberto Firmino sent a shot wide, Mane clattered the post with a powerful right-footed effort and Salah forced Ramsdale into another save, but in the midst of all that was an almighty scare.

Ryan Fraser got in behind the Reds' defence and lobbed Adrian, but James Milner – deputising at left-back for Andy Robertson – sprinted back to the goalline to volley clear.

That lunging clearance secured Liverpool's record-setting 22nd consecutive top-flight home win and, with Manchester City losing the Manchester derby the following day, left the Reds six points short of winning the title.

But Liverpool's march to title number 19 was about to be disrupted by Covid-19.

79

EVERTON 0
LIVERPOOL 0

21.06.20 • Goodison Park • Attendance: BCD
Referee: Mike Dean

EVERTON (4-4-2): Pickford, Coleman (C), Holgate, Keane, Digne, Iwobi (Bernard 87), Davies, Gomes, Gordon (Sigurdsson 60), Richarlison, Calvert-Lewin (Kean, 90).
Subs not used: Stekelenburg, Virginia, Baines, Martina, Branthwaite, Baningime.
Booked: Keane, Digne.

LIVERPOOL (4-3-3): Alisson, Alexander-Arnold, Matip (Lovren 73), van Dijk, Milner (Gomez 42), Henderson (C), Fabinho, Keita (Wijnaldum 65), Minamino (Oxlade-Chamberlain 46), Firmino (Origi 65), Mane.
Subs not used: Adrian, Salah, Elliott, Williams. Booked: Milner, Origi.

PRESS BOX:
DAVID MADDOCK, DAILY MIRROR
"It was perhaps fitting that Liverpool finally resumed their epic quest for the tittle on the weekend that marked the longest day in the British calendar. So, perhaps predictably, the longest wait to become champions must go on a little longer."

PUNDIT:
JAMIE CARRAGHER, SKY SPORTS
"Everton allowed Liverpool to have possession because they know they can't take them on in that type of game. It was easy for Liverpool to dominate possession, but when you get that much possession in the opposition's half, it's about what you can do with it."

EVERTON v LIVERPOOL

MANAGER: JÜRGEN KLOPP

"The point is the one we deserved, even when I have to admit that, of course, Everton had the biggest chance to win the game. That was a little bit our problem, that we didn't create enough chances with all the possession we had. When I think about it, all the derbies here at Goodison looked pretty similar."

FOR THE RECORD:

This was Jürgen Klopp's 11th consecutive Merseyside derby without defeat since the start of his Liverpool career, a new club record. Bob Paisley had also previously gone 10 undefeated.

ALSO THIS WEEKEND:

• Brighton & Hove Albion 2-1 Arsenal
• Tottenham Hotspur 1-1 Manchester United
• Manchester City 5-0 Burnley

REPORT:

The 236th Merseyside derby was unlike any other. For the first time in the history of both clubs, Liverpool and Everton played a competitive match behind closed doors.

Never had the Reds played a league game in June. Never had Liverpool played on Father's Day. But then never had English football been suspended for over three months due to a global pandemic.

At the start of the Covid-19 outbreak, Jürgen Klopp described football as "the most important of the least important things." For it to be safe for the players to return to action three months later was something to be thankful for, but football isn't the same without supporters inside stadiums.

That was evident at Goodison Park where a dull Merseyside derby was played in an eerie atmosphere with the shouts of the players and coaching staff only drowned out by a light aircraft flying overhead during the early exchanges.

Before kick-off, the lives lost to the deadly virus were remembered through a minute's silence. The lives saved, and the sacrifices made, by the country's incredible key workers were marked by NHS patches on the players' shirts.

The Black Lives Matter movement was also acknowledged on shirtsleeve patches before the powerful sight of all 22 players and the match officials 'taking the knee' was beamed into living rooms worldwide. Trent Alexander-Arnold had Black Lives Matter printed upon his boots, although Sadio Mane was so excited to get the season restarted that he sprinted forward when the first whistle went before remembering to take the knee.

With Mo Salah only fit enough to be on the bench and Andy Robertson missing through injury, Takumi Minamino made his first Premier League start and James Milner deputised at left-back. Milner was forced off before half-time with a hamstring problem and Alex Oxlade-Chamberlain replaced Minamino at the interval following a first half that Liverpool dominated without creating many chances.

Joel Matip headed an Alexander-Arnold free-kick wide and Roberto Firmino dragged a shot across Jordan Pickford's goal after a nice touch from Mane. At the other end Alisson was a spectator, but his class was required after the break.

Again the Reds were on top. The excellent Naby Keita volleyed wide and an Alexander-Arnold free-kick was deflected over, but it was Everton who had the best chances late on after Matip went off with a toe injury. Dominic Calvert-Lewin's flicked effort, from Richarlison's cross, was well saved by Alisson, before Joe Gomez deflected a Tom Davies' shot from the rebound against a post.

Calvert-Lewin headed a corner wide and Alisson blocked from Richarlison, but Fabinho almost snatched a stoppage-time winner only for Pickford to tip his free-kick over.

So, just like in the previous two seasons when supporters were present, the Goodison derby finished goalless, stretching Liverpool's unbeaten run against Everton to 22 games. There may have been no goals nor supporters, but at least the return of the Reds in a season that could have been declared null and void was something to celebrate.

W

LIVERPOOL 4
CRYSTAL PALACE 0

Goals: Alexander-Arnold (23), Salah (44), Fabinho (55), Mane (69)

24.06.20 • Anfield • Attendance: BCD
Referee: Martin Atkinson

LIVERPOOL (4-3-3): Alisson, Alexander-Arnold (Williams 74), Gomez, van Dijk, Robertson (Elliott 84), J Henderson (C) (Oxlade-Chamberlain 64), Fabinho, Wijnaldum, Salah, Firmino (Minamino 74), Mane (Keita 84).
Subs not used: Adrian, Lovren, Origi, Jones

CRYSTAL PALACE (4-1-4-1): Hennessey, Ward, Cahill (C), Sakho, van Aanholt, McCarthy, Townsend, Kouyate (Milivojevic 66), McArthur (Riedewald 66), Zaha (Meyer 15), Ayew (Pierrick 84). Subs not used: S Henderson, Dann, Tavares, Mitchell.

PRESS BOX:
JOHN MURRAY, BBC RADIO 5LIVE
"A match behind closed doors at Anfield is just a surreal experience. Football is not meant to be like this. You'd be forgiven for thinking this was played out in front of a full and raucous Anfield, though – Liverpool played some fantastic football."

PUNDIT:
JAMIE REDKNAPP, SKY SPORTS
"Trent Alexander-Arnold, at his age, taking free-kicks, corners...everything he has done, the assists he makes – he's just an exceptional footballer. He's got great technique and the way he got top-spin on that ball for his goal – you can't save that. It's pure brilliance and he just gets better all the time."

MANAGER: JÜRGEN KLOPP
"Imagine how this stadium would have been full today and all the people could have experienced it live. I don't think the game could have been better because my boys played like everybody was in the stadium. The atmosphere on the pitch was incredible."

FOR THE RECORD:
Trent Alexander-Arnold, aged 21 years and 261 days old, became the youngest LFC player to score a direct free-kick at Anfield since Robbie Fowler (20 years and 252 days old) v Manchester United in 1995.

ALSO THIS MIDWEEK:
• Chelsea 2-1 Manchester City
• Leicester City 0-0 Brighton & Hove Albion
• Manchester United 3-0 Sheffield United

REPORT:
For three decades, supporters of rival clubs kept count of how many years it had been between league titles for Liverpool FC. They said it would never be our year, that our days were numbered. At least they got the last bit right.

Call it a quirk. Call it coincidence. Call it fate. But if you add up the shirt numbers of Liverpool's four goalscorers – Trent Alexander-Arnold (66), Mo Salah (11), Fabinho (3) and Sadio Mane (10) – in this 4-0 Anfield win against Crystal Palace, you get 90. The year of LFC's last championship success.

Just 24 hours later, with Jürgen Klopp, his staff, players and all in the 'Melwood bubble' watching on TV together while enjoying a barbecue at Formby Hall Golf Resort, Manchester City had to win at Chelsea or Liverpool would be champions for the first time in 30 years.

When the final whistle blew at Stamford Bridge, with Pep Guardiola's side losing 2-1, there were 96 minutes on the clock – a poignant number that sends shivers down the spine when you think about it. And in that moment, as supporters of Liverpool Football Club looked on from every part of the planet, the explosion of both joy and relief was palpable. It was unlike any other.

→

83

LIVERPOOL v CRYSTAL PALACE

Thirty years of pent-up frustration and anguish. Released. Thirty years of hoping it would finally be our time again. Over. Thirty years of waiting for the Liver Bird to sit back on its perch. Finished. Liverpool, our Liverpool, were champions of England again.

For it to happen in June, on a night when Liverpool weren't even playing, in the midst of a world-changing global pandemic, only added to the surreal feeling. But for it to happen the night after Liverpool turned in arguably their best home performance of the entire season made it even more special.

Anfield may have been eerily empty for Crystal Palace's visit, but it didn't stop the Reds from playing champagne football. Nor did it stop the Kop from looking a vibrant picture of colour thanks to Liverpool supporters, led by the Spion Kop 1906 group, covering the seats with the best set of banners in the business.

Never before had Liverpool played a competitive game behind closed doors at Anfield, but hearing You'll Never Walk Alone played in its traditional spot before kick-off reminded the players that, as Jordan Henderson put it in his programme notes: "the fans haven't disappeared, they're just somewhere else. They still watch and they still support."

In the opening 20 minutes Gini Wijnaldum miscued a shot wide and Henderson fired over. Palace lost Wilfried Zaha to injury and Roberto Firmino had an effort saved. Then came the glorious opener.

Jordan Ayew fouled Virgil van Dijk on the edge of the box and up stepped Alexander-Arnold to curl a free-kick into the top corner. It was so precise that two goalkeepers wouldn't have saved it.

Roy Hodgson's side were now in trouble. Henderson struck a post and van Dijk's effort from the rebound was scrambled off the line by Joel Ward. The second goal was coming.

Fabinho, who ran the midfield all night, clipped a delightful pass forward that allowed Salah to run in behind Patrick van Aanholt, chest the ball down and slot it past Wayne Hennessey. Simple, but a sublime way to score Liverpool's 100th goal of the season.

Ten minutes after the interval, Fabinho got in on the goalscoring act himself. Andy Robertson nutmegged referee Martin Atkinson with a pass and, given time to take a touch, the Brazilian midfielder sent an absolute thunderbolt of a shot into the back of the Kop net.

Behind the goal, in the entrance to Block 107, the jacket of Paul Smith, steward 348, was hanging up. It was on display in memory of Paul, who lost his life to Covid-19, so it was fitting that a player who regularly sprints down the wing directly in front of block 107, when the Reds attack the Kop end, got Liverpool's fourth.

Mane won possession on the touchline in his own half and turned the ball to Firmino. He slipped it to Salah, who pinged a first-time diagonal pass with his right foot for Mane to run clear of the Eagles' defence. He took a touch and curled a low shot into the bottom corner for his sixth goal in his last six appearance against Crystal Palace.

Klopp's men could easily have netted a fifth. Salah's 90th minute cross, to substitute Takumi Minamino, was cut out by Hennessey to prevent a tap-in, while Neco Williams, brought on to make his Premier League debut, saw stoppage-time efforts blocked by ex-Red Mamadou Sakho and saved by Hennessey. Even so, the Reds' dominance wasn't just illustrated by the 4-0 final scoreline.

Liverpool didn't allow Crystal Palace a single touch in their penalty area, the first time a Premier League team hasn't done so since Opta began keeping records in 2008/09. Technically it made Alisson the only spectator in the ground...and then all eyes turned to Stamford Bridge.

→

Twenty-four hours later, following Manchester City's 2-1 defeat at Chelsea, Liverpool's domination of the entire Premier League season was confirmed when the Reds were crowned champions with seven games to play, a new top-flight record.

Never has a league title been more deserved and the celebrations lasted long into the night as the players sprayed champagne, bounced around to Robin S's dance anthem 'Show Me Love,' Gala's 'Freed From Desire' and sang You'll Never Walk Alone.

After giving a tearful interview to Sky Sports, when the enormity of ending Liverpool's 30-year wait to be champions left him feeling overwhelmed, Klopp later showed off a few moves on the dance floor. The following day, as it all began to sink in, Liverpool's Premier League winning manager reflected on his team's success.

"The whole ride is a wonderful experience, but especially last night," he told liverpoolfc.com. "It was very special. So many people would have deserved to be part of this last night. So many more people than there were last night. But we had to make decisions.

"We all had to make decisions and the decision was everybody who is at Melwood in the moment with us every day, and got tested twice, can be there, no other people. So we did it without families of course, we did it without the wives as well. It was just the team and the staff around, but that was the minimum that we had to do.

"I cannot imagine how it would have been had we been all alone at home. Yes, with our families, but still kind of alone and not with the players together, how that would have felt. So it was perfect. It was big, a big emotional moment. The final whistle was a big moment.

"I think it would have been appropriate to speak, but I couldn't. I just couldn't. I realised when I started doing the Sky TV interview when the tears came up and then I spoke to Ulla. I had no chance to say a word. I just cried and if I'd have spoken to the players they wouldn't understand me, so it was not the right moment.

"I have enough opportunities to tell the boys what I think about them and how thankful I am and how much I appreciate their effort they put in, the determination, desire, everything. But they should understand me in that moment and it was not possible last night."

Like so many Liverpool supporters, Klopp struggled to sleep afterwards. At 2.30am he lay in bed trying to comprehend how his team could be 23 points ahead of Manchester City, who had taken 198 points in the previous two campaigns, to win the Premier League with seven games in hand. And as he lay there, his mind buzzing, this was the conclusion he came to.

"It's just a mix of skill and attitude – and the absolute understanding of the needs of this club and the supporters," he said. "That's what this team is, they understand 100%.

"I thought a lot about what we did in the last few years and I think one of the most important things I said – I had no idea how important this was when I said it – was we have to write our own story and create our own history. Because that's what was necessary and that's what these boys have done now.

"This is an active thing, we created our own story and history and didn't try to do what our wonderful dads and grandfathers did with this club. That gave us the opportunity to feel free enough to do what the boys did.

"So I'm really, really happy for them because they were legends before that in my mind, but now they are real legends."

MANCHESTER CITY 4
LIVERPOOL 0

Goals: De Bruyne (25pen), Sterling (35), Foden (45), Oxlade-Chamberlain (66og)

02.07.20 • **Etihad Stadium** • **Attendance:** BCD
Referee: Anthony Taylor

MANCHESTER CITY (4-2-3-1): Ederson, Walker (Cancelo 73), Garcia, Laporte (Otamendi 79), Mendy, Gundogan, Rodri, Foden, De Bruyne (C), Sterling (B Silva 79), Jesus (Mahrez 58). Subs not used: Bravo, Stones, Zinchenko, D Silva, Doyle. Booked: Mendy, Walker.

LIVERPOOL (4-3-3): Alisson, Alexander-Arnold (Williams 76), Gomez (Oxlade-Chamberlain 46), van Dijk, Robertson, Henderson (C), Fabinho, Wijnaldum (Keita 62), Salah, Firmino (Origi 62), Mane (Minamino 85). Subs not used: Adrian, Milner, Jones, Elliott. Booked: Gomez, Henderson.

PRESS BOX:
JASON BURT, DAILY TELEGRAPH
"Liverpool have clearly enjoyed their title celebrations – and why not? – and, to be honest, there was zero jeopardy at stake, despite the opposition, given they kicked off with a crushing advantage and the swagger of being champions. At the final whistle the lead was down to 20 points which is still bigger than any between first and second in top-flight history."

PUNDIT:
ROY KEANE, SKY SPORTS
"They had chances and they were just lacking concentration. The effort was there and we watched the game live, and I think Liverpool's attitude was fine. No top manager likes to get beat 4-0. That's why they're champions. They're fuming to being beaten 4-0."

MANAGER: JÜRGEN KLOPP

"It was reminder how good Manchester City are. I didn't need that, it's true, I knew that before. But it was still a surprise that it is possible. It is nice that in a league that City play in, that someone else can still be champions with the quality they have. I saw tonight a team who are ready, my team were OK. But if we lose 4-0 you don't have many arguments."

FOR THE RECORD:

This was the first time Naby Keita has ever been on the losing side in a Premier League game in his 37th league appearance for Liverpool.

ALSO THIS MIDWEEK:

• West Ham United 3-2 Chelsea
• Sheffield United 3-1 Tottenham Hotspur
• Everton 2-1 Leicester City

REPORT:

Sometimes in football a result goes against you that weirdly puts what you have already achieved into perspective. Liverpool's 4-0 defeat at Manchester City was one of those occasions.

The Cityzens deserved to win. As Jürgen Klopp said afterwards, 5-3 rather than 4-0 would arguably have been a fairer reflection on a game in which the Reds had more possession and 11 shots on goal. Yet the fact that the Premier League champions can lose by four goals to their closest rivals, but still be 20 points above them, is true testament to Liverpool's outstanding season.

Statistically, having taken 198 points during the previous two seasons, Pep Guardiola's side are the best in the history of top-flight football. But despite this defeat Liverpool could still eclipse that tally by taking 201 points in a two-season period, including a new Premier League record of 104.

Irrespective of if that is achieved or not, finishing as champions is all that truly matters – but winning the league by finishing so far ahead of a side as good as Manchester City adds to the scale of the achievement.

Liverpool's only Premier League defeat in 2018/19 came at the Etihad. So if the Reds were going to suffer another reverse in their hardest away game of the season then what better time for it to occur than after they'd already won the title with seven games to play?

The guard of honour that City afforded to Klopp's champions as they walked out onto the pitch was a reminder that there has been a changing of the guard this season, but the final result also indicated what kind of challenge awaits Liverpool in 2020/21. Had the Reds taken their early chances, however, it may have been a different story.

Four minutes had been played when Mo Salah chested down Virgil van Dijk's exquisite pass and volleyed goalwards. Ederson dived to push the shot away, then managed to take the sting out of Roberto Firmino's effort from the rebound.

Salah came even closer in the 19th minute when he cut inside from Firmino's pass and struck a low shot against the foot of the post, Sadio Mane mis-controlling the rebound.

The Reds were on top, but were made to pay for not converting those opportunities – and wasting some other promising attacks – by a clinical City side led by the outstanding Kevin De Bruyne.

It was the Belgian who put the hosts ahead from the penalty spot in the 25th minute after Joe Gomez was adjudged to have fouled Raheem Sterling. Ex-Red Sterling then netted his first Premier League goal against Liverpool and on the stroke of half-time Phil Foden found space to make it 3-0.

A second half own goal from substitute Alex Oxlade-Chamberlain, who was trying to keep a Sterling shot out, completed the heaviest defeat suffered by Premier League champions since Liverpool beat Arsenal 4-0 at Anfield in 1998. But then you can only lose as champions when already champions in the first place, something Liverpool very much are.

LIVERPOOL v ASTON VILLA

GAME 33

LIVERPOOL 2
ASTON VILLA 0

Goals: Mane (71), Jones (89)

05.07.20 • Anfield • Attendance: BCD

Referee: Paul Tierney

LIVERPOOL (4-3-3): Alisson, Alexander-Arnold, Gomez, van Dijk (C), Robertson (Williams 90), Oxlade-Chamberlain (Wijnaldum 61), Fabinho (Henderson 61), Keita (Jones 85), Salah, Origi (Firmino 61), Mane. Subs not used: Adrian, Minamino, Shaqiri, Elliott. Booked: Robertson.

ASTON VILLA (4-4-1-1): Reina, Konsa, Hause, Mings, Taylor, El Ghazi (Jota 74), Luiz, McGinn, Trezeguet (Vassilev 85), Grealish (C), Davis (Samatta 74). Subs not used: Nyland, Lansbury, Nakamba, Hourihane, Guilbert, Elmohamady. Booked: McGinn.

PRESS BOX:

DAVID LYNCH, LONDON EVENING STANDARD

"Adam Lallana's departure on a free transfer is expected to open up opportunities for Curtis Jones, and he showed that he is ready to take on that mantle with a maiden Premier League goal that required a perfectly timed arrival into the box and a cool finish. What a week for the teenager."

PUNDIT:

GERARD HOULLIER, LIVERPOOL ECHO

"Naby Keita was playing for a 'Championship' team in France. They were struggling, but he was playing everyone off the park. Like when I saw Steven Gerrard, he was practically everywhere and his maturity was impressive, even under pressure. Once he fits in the team, he will stay there."

REPORT:

The last time Pepe Reina played against Liverpool at Anfield, Curtis Jones was two-and-a-half months old. Reina was an 18-year-old goalkeeper with Barcelona at the time, playing in the second leg of the UEFA Cup semi-final.

Nineteen years later, 37-year-old Reina faced the Reds at Anfield once more and found himself beaten by 19-year-old Jones. For a face of Liverpool's past to concede a goal to a face of Liverpool's future, in the club's first home game as champions for 30 years, somehow felt symbolic.

That such a moment didn't occur in front of a packed Kop was a shame, and not just for Liverpool supporters.

It was a shame for Reina, who made the last of his 394 appearances for the Reds in May 2013 and would have received a rapturous reception as he ran towards the Kop at the start of the second half. And a shame for Jones who, a day after signing a contract extension, scored his first Premier League goal and didn't get to experience Anfield's adulation when the ball hit the net.

Had this game been played in its original slot in April everything would have been different. Who is to say Jones and Reina would even have been on the pitch? But at a time when football has to be played without fans present, it is hard not to think of what might have been.

At least Liverpool supporters had provided a couple of welcome new additions to Anfield. Stretching across the upper tier of the Sir Kenny Dalglish stand was a new banner – 'LIVERPOOL FC – CHAMPIONS AGAIN' – with a similar one displayed on the Kop.

Incredibly, since it was announced that the Centenary Stand would

90

MANAGER: JÜRGEN KLOPP

"If we want to have a record points tally we pretty much have to win all the football games so it's not that complicated. I don't have to mention it, the boys know that. But it's not necessary for this group. You get three points if you win and that's enough."

FOR THE RECORD:

Curtis Jones was the 17th different league goalscorer for Liverpool this season, equalling the club record set in 1911/12 and 2015/16.

ALSO THIS WEEKEND:

- Southampton 1-0 Manchester City
- Tottenham Hotspur 1-0 Everton
- Wolverhampton Wanderers 0-2 Arsenal

be renamed after King Kenny in May 2017, the Reds haven't lost a Premier League game at Anfield and they stretched that unbeaten run to a whopping 57 games with this 2-0 win against Aston Villa.

It was also Liverpool's 17th home league win from 17 games. No team has won all 19 home fixtures in a Premier League season before and the 51 points taken at Anfield so far would put the Reds seventh in the table, a point above Arsenal.

Not that anyone will care to remember the first half. Villa afforded Liverpool a guard of honour as the champions emerged from the tunnel, but Divock Origi's new bleach-blond haircut was the most striking feature of a tepid 45 minutes.

The 60th minute arrival of substitutes Jordan Henderson, Gini Wijnaldum and Roberto Firmino livened things up. Ten minutes later

the Reds were ahead when Trent Alexander-Arnold and Naby Keita combined to tee up Sadio Mane, who slammed the ball in off the underside of the crossbar for his 50th goal at Anfield.

Jones then struck in the 89th minute, his shot from Mo Salah's knockdown clipping Tyrone Mings on the way in, before Alisson preserved another clean sheet with a superb save from Jack Grealish.

It won't be Jones' last goal for the champions, but it may be the last Anfield sees of Pepe Reina.

REPORT:

When Liverpool were confirmed as Premier League champions with seven games to spare, questions were raised about what happens next?

Would Jürgen Klopp's side lose their intensity? Would they still counter-press like the world depended on it? Would their passing be passive? History suggested a drop in performances and results was likely.

In 1982/83, Bob Paisley's Reds needed one point from their final six games to be champions – and one point is all they took. After streaking clear they faded, winning the league with a 2-0 loss at Spurs – after title-rivals Manchester United dropped points – amidst their worst run of defeats for 18 years.

Kenny Dalglish's class of 1987/88 also won the title early against Tottenham, this time with a 1-0 victory, but then lost their momentum, winning just one of their final four league games and losing the FA Cup final to Wimbledon.

So, for 2019/20 Premier League champions Liverpool to go 2-0 up at Brighton in the opening eight minutes, due to two goals directly created by their trademark counter-pressing, was a reminder of their relentless mentality.

They'd already won the league, but showed they would try to chase records. And Brighton players with the ball.

Graham Potter's Seagulls like to play out from the back, but with Naby Keita buzzing around the midfield it was an ill-advised policy.

Six minutes had been played when Keita robbed Davy Propper of possession, just outside his own penalty area, and slipped a pass to his right. Roberto Firmino had the vision to let the ball roll to Mo Salah, who whipped a first-time shot past Mat Ryan.

Within 127 seconds it was 2-0. Jordan Henderson pressed Adam Webster, who gave the ball to Keita. He found Firmino, who fed Salah, and when the Egyptian touched the ball back it was to Jordan Henderson, who clipped a brilliant first-time shot past Ryan from almost 25 yards out.

Forget easing up, it was the first time Liverpool had scored twice in the opening eight minutes of a league game since doing so at Fulham in 2011.

Neco Williams, playing at left-back on his first Premier League start, made a sliding block to deny Leandro Trossard as Brighton responded. And it was Trossard who pulled a goal back shortly before half-time when he volleyed home Tariq Lamptey's cross.

Ryan denied Salah in a one-on-one early in the second half before Gini Wijnaldum cleared from in front of his own goalline when Dan Burn fluffed a golden opportunity to level. Virgil van Dijk also remarkably stopped one attack by heading the ball clear to himself, clips of it going viral online.

The Seagulls were made to pay when Salah dashed to the near post to head in a corner from Andy Robertson, on at half-time for the booked Williams, to make it 3-1.

Salah should have completed his hat-trick in stoppage-time, but saw Ryan tip a shot over and then headed over himself. It mattered not. Liverpool had a club record-equalling 30th league win – and 13th away win – of a season that only had records left to play for.

BRIGHTON & HOVE ALBION 1
LIVERPOOL 3
Goals: Trossard (45); Salah (6, 76), Henderson (8)
08.07.20 • AMEX Stadium • Attendance: BCD
Referee: Craig Pawson

BRIGHTON & HOVE ALBION (4-3-1-2): Ryan, Lamptey, Webster, Dunk (C), Burn, Propper (Bissouma 71), Stephens, Mac Allister (Mooy 71), Gross (Connolly 71), Maupay, Trossard. Subs not used: Button, Duffy, Jahanbakhsh, Murray, Montoya, Bernardo. Booked: Lamptey.

LIVERPOOL (4-3-3): Alisson, Alexander-Arnold, Gomez, van Dijk, Williams (Robertson 46), Keita (Fabinho 61), Henderson (C) (Milner 80), Wijnaldum, Salah, Firmino (Minamino 87), Oxlade-Chamberlain (Mane 61). Subs not used: Adrian, Origi, Jones, Elliott. Booked: Williams, Mane, Fabinho, Gomez.

PRESS BOX:
JOHN CROSS, DAILY MIRROR

"It has become the longest victory tour. Newly-crowned champions Liverpool were given another guard of honour, they edged closer to another Premier League record, and Mo Salah turned on the style. With the title long since wrapped up, this feels like the Harlem Globetrotters going round the country playing exhibition matches."

PUNDIT:
MATT MURRAY, SKY SPORTS

"You know that Liverpool love to press and you know they are going to be diligent in their game plan and set the traps. When they get into those positions, with Brighton being so expansive, they are going to be clinical. Brighton learned that the hard way in the first eight minutes because they were 2-0 down."

MANAGER: JÜRGEN KLOPP

"I saw two very good teams, both trying to play football. We are champions and it could be softening, but it is not – the boys go with everything. We have 92 points and last season we had 97. We got five points more than this last season – that's unbelievable, I have no idea how we did that!"

FOR THE RECORD:
Mo Salah's two goals and an assist took him to 100 goal involvements (73 goals, 27 assists) in 104 Premier League appearances for Liverpool.

ALSO THIS MIDWEEK:
• Manchester City 5-0 Newcastle United
• Arsenal 1-1 Leicester City
• Sheffield United 1-0 Wolverhampton Wanderers

LIVERPOOL v BURNLEY

LIVERPOOL 1
BURNLEY 1

Goals: Robertson (34); Rodriguez (69)
11.07.20 • Anfield • **Attendance:** BCD
Referee: David Coote

LIVERPOOL (4-3-3): Alisson, Williams (Alexander-Arnold 69), Gomez, van Dijk (C), Robertson, Wijnaldum (Oxlade-Chamberlain 81), Fabinho, Jones (Keita 69), Salah, Firmino, Mane. Subs not used: Adrian, Lovren, Minamino, Shaqiri, Origi, Elliott. Booked: Gomez.

BURNLEY (4-4-2): Pope, Bardsley, Long, Tarkowski (C), Taylor, Pieters (Gudmundsson 65), Westwood, Brownhill, McNeil, Wood (Vydra 65), Rodriguez. Subs not used: Peacock-Farrell, Brady, Thompson, Dunne, Benson, Goodridge, Driscoll-Glennon. Booked: Bardsley, Pope.

PRESS BOX:
ANDY HUNTER, THE GUARDIAN
"Nick Pope was inspired and the main reason the champions' run of 24 consecutive home league wins is over. Liverpool were aiming to become the first top-flight team since Sunderland in 1891/92 to complete a campaign with a 100% home record but Burnley's organisation, strength and rousing finish put paid to that."

PUNDIT:
DANNY MURPHY, BBC MATCH OF THE DAY
"I was really impressed with Curtis Jones. He plays in midfield, he's going to score goals. He gets in there, times his runs beautifully, he's comfortable with both feet and knows when to pass and when to dribble. He showed all of the bits of quality you need to play at this level."

MANAGER: JÜRGEN KLOPP
"For moments it was Liverpool against Pope, he did really well. We did everything right and he made saves but we should have scored more, that's on us. I think it's the biggest challenge in football to create against a team that is that well organised and has such an outstanding attitude like Burnley has. We didn't close the game and they took their moment. I can't deny it feels like we've lost the game."

FOR THE RECORD:
This was the first league game all season that the Reds have failed to win after scoring the opening goal, having won the previous 27 when going ahead.

ALSO THIS WEEKEND:
• Sheffield United 3-0 Chelsea
• Bournemouth 4-1 Leicester City
• Manchester United 2-2 Southampton

REPORT:
Having won all 17 league games at Anfield, the champions were aiming to become the first team since Liverpool Football Club was formed in 1892 to complete a top-flight campaign with a 100% home record. Some divine interventions from Burnley's Pope – Nick Pope – ended that dream.

The Clarets' keeper made eight saves over the course of the 90 minutes, two of them world class, to keep Burnley alive when they could have been on the end of a first-half pummelling.

His first save came from Curtis Jones, making his first Premier League start, in the 17th minute. Moments later he somehow clawed Mo Salah's volley out from underneath the crossbar.

Pope used his feet to deny Salah in the 33rd minute, but from the resulting corner the Reds found a way through. Andy Robertson's corner was cleared, but Virgil van Dijk kept the ball in play and Jones slipped it to Fabinho on the edge of the box.

Still out on the right after taking the corner, Robertson made a darting, diagonal run into the box. Fabinho clipped a perfectly-weighted cross towards him and the Scot met it with a glorious header that arced beyond Pope as he dived at full-stretch.

It was Robertson's second goal of the season, both headers against teams that play in claret.

On the stroke of half-time Salah turned provider when he sublimely controlled Robertson's cross and played a neat pass to Sadio Mane. The Senegalese striker beat Kevin Long on the turn and fired goalwards, but Pope flung himself to his right to tip the ball over.

Had Burnley boss Sean Dyche thrown the kitchen sink at his players during the half-time interval Pope would probably have turned that around the dressing-room door too, such was the form he was in.

Roberto Firmino did manage to beat him four minutes after the interval, but the inside of the post denied the Brazilian that elusive first Premier League goal of the season at Anfield. Jones then fired wide, after a neat one-two with Salah, before the Reds were caught out in the immediate aftermath of the second half water break.

Mane was wrongly flagged offside in the 67th minute and, before the action resumed, referee David Coote, on his Anfield debut, blew for the water break. Trent Alexander-Arnold and Naby Keita were both brought on, and Burnley restarted by launching a long free-kick into the Liverpool penalty area that James Tarkowski headed down for Jay Rodriguez to hook home on the half-volley.

The Reds rallied. Alexander-Arnold had a shot pawed out by Pope and Robertson was brought down in the Burnley box by Johann Gudmundsson, but no penalty was awarded.

Gudmundsson then almost gave the visitors the ultimate smash-and-grab win when Alisson's punch fell to the Icelandic international, but he rattled the crossbar.

One final opportunity came Liverpool's way in stoppage time when Alexander-Arnold crossed for Salah, but again the ball ended up in the arms of Pope – the first man to stop the champions winning a league game at Anfield all season.

ARSENAL 2
LIVERPOOL 1

Goals: Lacazette (32), Nelson (44); Mane (20)
15.07.20 • Emirates Stadium • Attendance: BCD
Referee: Paul Tierney

PRESS BOX:
MARTIN SAMUEL, DAILY MAIL
"Perhaps Liverpool were just too good, their supremacy too apparent from way out. On average, Premier League champions accrue 0.5 points per game fewer once the deed is done – and Liverpool have had further to travel with their feet up than any team in history."

PUNDIT:
GRAEME SOUNESS, SKY SPORTS
"We won the league with five games to go, in Bob Paisley's last year, then lost four. In the last game of the season, at home to Aston Villa, we were saying to each other 'we've got to win this, this is his last game'. We scraped a draw. Don't ask me to explain it, but it happens. It's one or two per cent in concentration, allowing yourself to drift."

ARSENAL (3-4-3): Martinez, Holding, Luiz, Tierney, Soares (Maitland-Niles 76), Torreira (Ceballos 57), Xhaka, Saka (Kolasinac 57), Nelson (Aubameyang 58), Lacazette (C) (Willock 57), Pepe. Subs not used: Macey, Bellerin, Sokratis, Mustafi. Booked: Torreira, Ceballos, Xhaka.

LIVERPOOL (4-3-3): Alisson, Alexander-Arnold, Gomez, van Dijk (C), Robertson, Oxlade-Chamberlain (Keita 61), Fabinho, Wijnaldum (Shaqiri 83), Salah (Origi 83), Firmino (Minamino 61), Mane. Subs not used: Adrian, Lovren, Jones, Elliott, Williams. Booked: Alexander-Arnold.

MANAGER: JÜRGEN KLOPP

"I can't make something negative from something so positive, we get the points we deserve and we will see how many that will be. These boys played an exceptional season, nobody can take that away from them."

FOR THE RECORD:

Divock Origi came on to make his 82nd appearance as a substitute for Liverpool, one more than the previous club record of 81 held by Ryan Babel.

ALSO THIS MIDWEEK:

• Chelsea 1-0 Norwich City
• Manchester City 2-1 Bournemouth
• Newcastle United 1-3 Tottenham Hotspur

REPORT:

Facing the TV cameras when you've made a mistake in a game that Liverpool lose is something most players would rather avoid. So if you want an example of leadership in football look no further than Virgil van Dijk fronting up to do a live post-match interview following this 2-1 defeat at Arsenal.

With captain Jordan Henderson and vice-captain James Milner both absent through injury, van Dijk wore the armband. But even the best can make mistakes and it was from the Dutch international's stray pass that Alexandre Lacazette went around Alisson to make it 1-1 following Sadio Mane's opener.

An equally rare error by Alisson, who also passed to Lacazette to tee up Reiss Nelson, gifted the Gunners their winner. Awkward. Yet rather than go hiding in the dressing-room afterwards, van Dijk stayed pitchside and took full responsibility for Liverpool's first defeat to Arsenal since 2015.

"Until I made a mistake, there was nothing wrong," he told Sky Sports. "We played well, I had a feeling we could win here comfortably at one point, but obviously if you give them the goals you see what happens. Unfortunately I made the mistake, I take the blame for it of course. I take it as a man and we move on."

Alisson also took responsibility by facing the cameras for an interview with LFCTV.

"Maybe tonight we didn't deliver everything we have, maybe the mental aspect wasn't at 100%. We started to commit silly mistakes and then we committed two individual mistakes we're not used to committing during the season. Then we weren't there to cover those mistakes."

For both players to make goal-costing errors was rare, let alone in the same game, but it proved to be decisive on a night when Liverpool were again much the better team, but couldn't turn possession and pressure into goals.

Roberto Firmino often performs a 'kung-fu kick' celebration when team-mates score and he almost found the net in the 12th minute by jumping in front of Gunners goalkeeper Emiliano Martinez in such a manner. Martinez' clearance stuck Firmino's flying foot, but the ball cannoned wide off the post.

Firmino was involved in the opening goal seven minutes later. From his pass, Andy Robertson crossed low and the en-rushing Mane provided a first-time finish.

Then came the goal-costing errors. Under a challenge from Nelson, van Dijk presented the ball to Lacazette to equalise, and from Robertson's throw-in Alisson only found Lacazette, who set up Nelson to score. Not since April 2017 had the Reds lost in the Premier League when scoring first, but they couldn't find an equaliser.

Martinez did well to tip over from Mo Salah after some mesmerising footwork left David Luiz on his backside.

Substitute Takumi Minamino dragged a shot across goal and Mane flashed a late effort past the near post, but champions Liverpool were beaten for just a third time all season – ending their hopes of setting a new record Premier League points tally of over 100.

LIVERPOOL v CHELSEA

LIVERPOOL 5
CHELSEA 3

Goals: Keita (23), Alexander-Arnold (38), Wijnaldum (43), Firmino (54), Oxlade-Chamberlain (84); Giroud (45), Abraham (61), Pulisic (73)

22.07.20 • Anfield • Attendance: BCD

Referee: Andre Marriner

LIVERPOOL (4-3-3): Alisson, Alexander-Arnold, Gomez, van Dijk (C), Robertson, Keita (Jones 66), Fabinho, Wijnaldum (Milner 66), Salah (Oxlade-Chamberlain 79), Firmino (Minamino 87), Mane (Origi 87). Subs not used: Adrian, Lovren, Lallana, Shaqiri. Booked: Gomez.

CHELSEA (3-4-2-1): Arrizabalaga, Azpilicueta, Zouma, Rudiger, James, Jorginho, Kovacic, Alonso (Emerson 88), Willian (Pulisic 59), Giroud (Abraham 59), Mount (Hudson-Odoi 59). Subs not used: Caballero, Christensen, Pedro, Loftus-Cheek, Tomori.

PRESS BOX:
CHRIS BASCOMBE, DAILY TELEGRAPH
"Treading where nine Liverpool captains have gone before, Jordan Henderson could only guess the passion of the millions viewing. The placing of the temporary structure on the Kop meant he could absorb the spirit of the famous stand. One small step for a modest Wearsider, one giant leap for Liverpool's global fanbase."

PUNDIT:
JOHN BARNES, SKY SPORTS
"It has been a two-year journey. Last year they lost one game and won the Champions League, and this year with what they have done. To win 5-3 tonight, and play the way they did, was sensational. The level of consistency, the dynamism and the togetherness – everyone has come together to make this special moment."

MANAGER: JÜRGEN KLOPP
"We don't compare as we haven't won it before. It could have been better and we know that and it could have been worse if we had not won. These boys are so special. I couldn't be more proud of them throwing in a performance like this tonight on the pitch in an open game, obviously, but nice, nice goals. Incredible goals, super football in moments and I loved the game."

FOR THE RECORD:
This was the first time eight goals had been scored in a Premier League match at Anfield since a 4-4 draw against Arsenal in 2009.

ALSO THIS MIDWEEK:
• Watford 0-4 Manchester City
• Aston Villa 1-0 Arsenal
• Manchester United 1-1 West Ham United

REPORT:
Tonight was the night. The night when after 30 years and two months – and a total of 1,155 league games – Liverpool FC were finally presented with the trophy that symbolises being champions of England. Again.

Back in 1990, on a Tuesday night against Derby County, it was the old Football League Championship trophy that captain Alan Hansen raised aloft on the Anfield pitch. Tonight, on a specially constructed podium on the Kop, Jordan Henderson became the first Liverpool skipper to get his hands on the Premier League trophy. But first the champions had a game of football to play.

"As much as the 90 minutes is the main focus, I cannot ignore the hugely significant night we are about to experience as a team and a club," Jürgen Klopp wrote in his matchday programme notes.

"We have enjoyed a wonderful season and it is important we finish it in a manner fitting of the achievement. When the game is done, we will be recognised as the Champions of England. The first time since 1990 for this incredible football club. It is so important to enjoy the wonderful moments when they come. And this is one of those."

| LIVERPOOL FC | 5 | 22:06 |
| CHELSEA | 3 | 90:00 |

His Liverpool team certainly finished their record-equalling Anfield campaign in a manner fitting of champions. They played some outstanding football against a good Chelsea side on a night when the intensity level on the pitch was arguably the highest since football returned in June.

After sussing each other out during the opening 20 minutes like it was a giant game of chess, Naby Keita exploded into life long before the incredible pyro display that followed when the trophy was lifted.

Keita had already sent Cesar Azpilicueta for an Echo with one outrageous turn and dribble, but in the 23rd minute he hounded Willian out of possession, took a touch and blasted a shot goalwards that crashed into the net off the underside of the crossbar. What a hit, Naby lad.

Mason Mount had a goal disallowed for offside before Sadio Mane was fouled on the edge of the Chelsea box, sparking some friction between the two benches. Trent Alexander-Arnold stepped up and, just like he did at Stamford Bridge back in September, curled a magnificent free-kick into the top corner. Kepa Arrizabalaga didn't even dive.

A couple of minutes before half-time it was 3-0. Andy Robertson's corner appeared to be handled by Jorginho, but as Mo Salah appealed for a penalty he also flicked the ball to Gini Wijnaldum, who volleyed home. It was Liverpool's 50th Premier League goal of the season at Anfield and the first time the Reds had struck half-a-century of home league goals in consecutive campaigns since 1983/84.

Olivier Giroud pulled a goal back before the interval, sliding the ball home after Alisson had palmed Willian's shot into the air, before Salah missed a couple of good early second half opportunities to score against his old club. Then came a special moment.

Goalkeepers, defenders, the woodwork and VAR had all denied Roberto Firmino an Anfield league goal in 2019/20, but finally his time came in the 54th minute. Alexander-Arnold's cross from the right was perfect for an en-rushing forward to head home, which is precisely what Liverpool's Bobby Dazzler did in front of the Kop podium. Out came the kung-fu kick celebration before the Brazilian's delighted team-mates mobbed him.

The arrival of Chelsea substitute Christian Pulisic got them back into the game. The American forward set up Tammy Abraham to make it 4-2 following a mazy dribble, fired a golden opportunity wide and made the most of Virgil van Dijk and Joe Gomez colliding with one another to strike a shot into the top corner.

All of a sudden, the point Chelsea needed to secure Champions League qualification seemed achievable, but as fireworks let off outside echoed around Anfield, the Reds made it 5-3 with a thrilling goal on the counter-attack.

Robertson headed a Reece James free-kick clear at the near post. Within seconds the left-back had made a lung-busting diagonal run across the pitch to run onto a Mane pass and gone flying past Jorginho. The Scot then sent in a low cross that Curtis Jones let run behind him to fellow substitute Alex Oxlade-Chamberlain, who lifted a first-time, side-footed effort into the roof of the net.

It was a glorious way to end a glorious Anfield campaign with Liverpool's 18th win from 19 games both equalling the Premier League record and setting a new club achievement of three consecutive seasons without a league defeat at home. But then it's good to have a fortress when you've got the Holy Grail sat inside.

For Liverpool supporters to not be allowed inside Anfield to share the crowning moment was devastating, not just for every Red but for Klopp and his players too. Yet the Liverpool manager always seems to find the right words in any situation. "That's how life is," he told Sky

Champions 19/2

Sports' Kelly Cates on the Anfield pitch. "You make the best of what you get."

Lifting the Premier League trophy on the Kop, the pulsating heartbeat of Liverpool Football Club, after it had been handed over by Sir Kenny Dalglish – a man who epitomises this football club more than any other – was as good as it could possibly get under the circumstances.

King Kenny and Klopp on the Kop together. Embracing in a hug with the Premier League trophy, freshly engraved and sporting the reddest of all ribbons, placed next to them on the most famous stand in football. Emotional or what? Now bring on the champions.

The Liverpool manager was the first to hang a golden Premier League winners' medal around his neck. His immediate first-team coaching staff followed and then, one by one, so did his players, starting with Andy Lonergan, Caoimhin Kelleher and 17-year-old Harvey Elliott, who hadn't played enough games to qualify for guaranteed medals.

Then, with smoke pumped into the Kop and lighting making it glow red as Kanye West's All of the Lights was played, came the 23 men who will forever enjoy legendary status for ending a 30-year wait to win what Bill Shankly called "our bread and butter" – the league title.

Alisson. Adrian. Virgil van Dijk. Roberto Firmino. Fabinho. Gini Wijnaldum. Sadio Mane. Naby Keita. Joe Gomez. Divock Origi. Alex Oxlade-Chamberlain. Trent Alexander-Arnold. Andy Robertson. James Milner. Adam Lallana. Dejan Lovren. Mo Salah. Joel Matip. Takumi Minamino. Xherdan Shaqiri. Neco Williams. Curtis Jones. In that order.

Finally, a man Sir Kenny had signed, the soon-to-be-named FWA Footballer of the Year Jordan Henderson, walked up the steps, collected his medal and placed his hands and lips on the Premier League trophy. One kiss is all it takes.

He carried it towards his manager and team-mates – each waving their arms and shouting in anticipation – did his trademark Hendo Shuffle and turned to face the pitch before lifting the glittering silver trophy, complete with golden crown and golden lions, high into the air as Coldplay's A Sky Full of Stars rang out amidst a monsoon of red and silver ticker tape.

No pyro, no party, and as Liverpool's jubilant players bounced around the podium singing 'campiones, campiones, ole, ole, ole,' the sky above Anfield turned red with a spectacular fireworks display that could be seen for miles. Images representing the Owen McVeigh Foundation and Fans Supporting Foodbanks were also beamed onto the pitch as a reminder that even in moments of celebration, those we have lost, and those we can help, are not forgotten.

The players then joined the rest of the backroom staff on the pitch and lined up, their arms around one another, to sing You'll Never Walk Alone, many wearing scarves to represent the Liverpool supporters who couldn't be present. To have finished on 96 points was also poignant.

"It was absolutely great, absolutely great," said Klopp after carrying the Premier League trophy down the Anfield tunnel looking like the proudest man on the planet.

"I have to say, the people who organised it made the best of it. If it would have been the last game – win today and we are champions – then we wouldn't have had the opportunity to go on the Kop.

"I was never on the Kop before, it was pretty special and I think it makes sense in the moment when the people are not in that we use the Kop to celebrate it with them together in our hearts. It was really good."

Tonight was the night. Not the night Liverpool supporters could had envisaged back in August, but a glorious night when the mighty Reds finally lifted the Premier League trophy as champions.

Boom!

NEWCASTLE UNITED v LIVERPOOL

NEWCASTLE UNITED 1
LIVERPOOL 3

Goals: Gayle (1); van Dijk (38), Origi (59), Mane (89)
26.07.20 • St James' Park • Attendance: BCD
Referee: Anthony Taylor

NEWCASTLE UNITED (3-5-2): Dubravka, Manquillo, Fernandez, Rose (Watts 74), Lazaro, Shelvey (C), Bentaleb (S Longstaff 49), Almiron (Hayden 70), Ritchie, Saint-Maximin (Joelinton 46), Gayle (Carroll 70). Subs not used: Darlow, Muto, Yedlin, Young. Booked: Fernandez

LIVERPOOL (4-3-3): Alisson, Williams (Alexander-Arnold 85), Gomez, van Dijk, Robertson, Keita (Jones 85), Wijnaldum, Milner (C), Oxlade-Chamberlain (Firmino 64), Origi (Salah 64), Minamino (Mane 64). Subs not used: Adrian, Fabinho, Shaqiri, Elliott.

PRESS BOX:
PAUL GORST, LIVERPOOL ECHO
"So how to surmise a Premier League season that lasted a whopping 352 days? A campaign unlike any other, for so many reasons. Not least that it was Liverpool's name on the trophy when the dust settled and smoke cleared. It was nothing less than they deserve, too. They saw the job through. Liverpool are the champions of England. The best team around, bar none."

PUNDIT:
STEVE MCMANAMAN, BT SPORT
"It's hard for the starting eleven to get better. It's difficult when you are the world champions and won everything to get better when it comes to your starting eleven. I certainly think the squad can improve. It's going to be hard to displace the starting eleven, though."

MANAGER: JÜRGEN KLOPP
"The football part of the year was exceptional, absolutely exceptional, 99 points. The European Super Cup, the Club World Cup and now the Premier League is absolutely exceptional. Ninety-nine points after having 97 last year, absolutely exceptional. The boys showed a consistency that is really second to none and that's what we had to do, we knew that."

FOR THE RECORD:
Liverpool started a Premier League game without Mo Salah, Sadio Mane or Roberto Firmino in the starting XI for only the second time since Salah joined the Reds in 2017.

ALSO THIS WEEKEND:
• Everton 1-3 Bournemouth
• Arsenal 3-2 Watford
• West Ham United 1-1 Aston Villa

REPORT:
In a season when they have broken so many records, it was fitting that Liverpool ended an historic 2019/20 campaign by adding to their achievements.

This 3-1 victory at St James' Park took Liverpool to 99 points – not only a new club record, but the second highest total in the history of English football. Add it to the 97 points the Reds collected when finishing second last season and Jürgen Klopp's men have taken 196 points from a possible 228 in two years. Wow!

Never before has a Liverpool team been so consistent. Never before has a Liverpool team won 14 away games in a top-flight season either, but that can now be added to a bulging book of records thanks to goals from Virgil van Dijk, Divock Origi and Sadio Mane.

Another record was set in the opening minute when Newcastle went ahead. Ex-Reds' midfielder Jonjo Shelvey's quickly taken free-kick sent Dwight Gayle scurrying clear to beat Alisson with just 26 seconds on the clock. It was the earliest Premier League goal Liverpool have ever conceded, although it took VAR over two minutes to confirm that Gayle was onside.

Incredibly, the Magpies didn't touch the ball in the Reds' penalty area again until the second half, by which time Liverpool were in charge. Takumi Minamino, on his second Premier League start, forced Martin Dubravka to push a shot from distance just wide of the post, but it was van Dijk who provided the 38th minute equaliser.

Newcastle cleared a set piece, but the Reds kept the pressure on and when Alex Oxlade-Chamberlain beat Danny Rose down the right and crossed to the far post, van Dijk rose highest to loop a header into the net. It was Virgil's fifth goal of a second consecutive season in which he played in all 38 league games. He didn't miss a single minute, either.

Andy Robertson created the second in the 59th minute with his 12th Premier League assist – a new personal best – of the season. Robertson was the furthest Liverpool player forward when he knocked van Dijk's pass back to Origi. The Belgian striker cut inside from the left and, from just outside the penalty area, struck a powerful shot into the bottom corner.

The last thing Steve Bruce must have wanted to see five minutes later was Roberto Firmino, Sadio Mane and Mo Salah coming on, and they all meant business. Salah rattled the post with a shot from just his second touch and shortly after was played through by Firmino only for Federico Fernandez to deny him a 20th league goal of the season with a last-ditch sliding challenge.

Mane put the icing on the cake in the 89th minute. Running onto another pass from Firmino, he cut inside the penalty area, jinked past Valentino Lazaro and curled a spinning shot into the far corner.

Salah, arriving at the far post, simply stood there and applauded – something every Liverpool supporter will do loudly when finally allowed back inside Anfield to cheer their team of record breaking champions.

What a team. What a season.

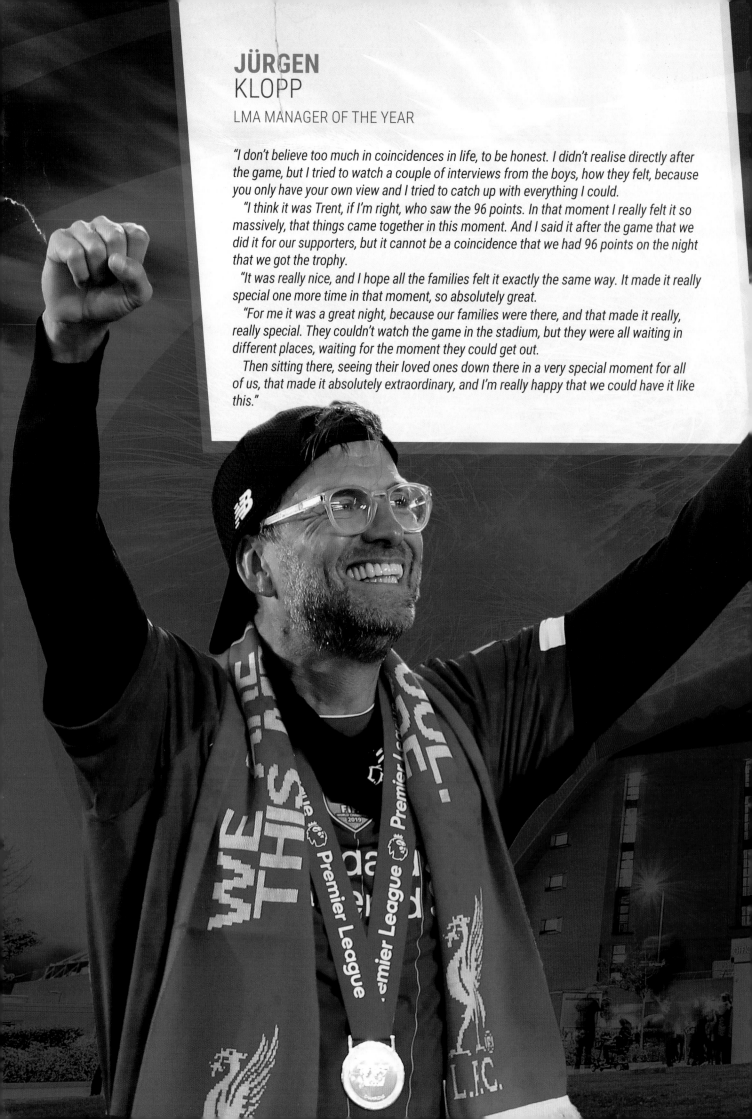

JÜRGEN
KLOPP

LMA MANAGER OF THE YEAR

"I don't believe too much in coincidences in life, to be honest. I didn't realise directly after the game, but I tried to watch a couple of interviews from the boys, how they felt, because you only have your own view and I tried to catch up with everything I could.

"I think it was Trent, if I'm right, who saw the 96 points. In that moment I really felt it so massively, that things came together in this moment. And I said it after the game that we did it for our supporters, but it cannot be a coincidence that we had 96 points on the night that we got the trophy.

"It was really nice, and I hope all the families felt it exactly the same way. It made it really special one more time in that moment, so absolutely great.

"For me it was a great night, because our families were there, and that made it really, really special. They couldn't watch the game in the stadium, but they were all waiting in different places, waiting for the moment they could get out.

Then sitting there, seeing their loved ones down there in a very special moment for all of us, that made it absolutely extraordinary, and I'm really happy that we could have it like this."

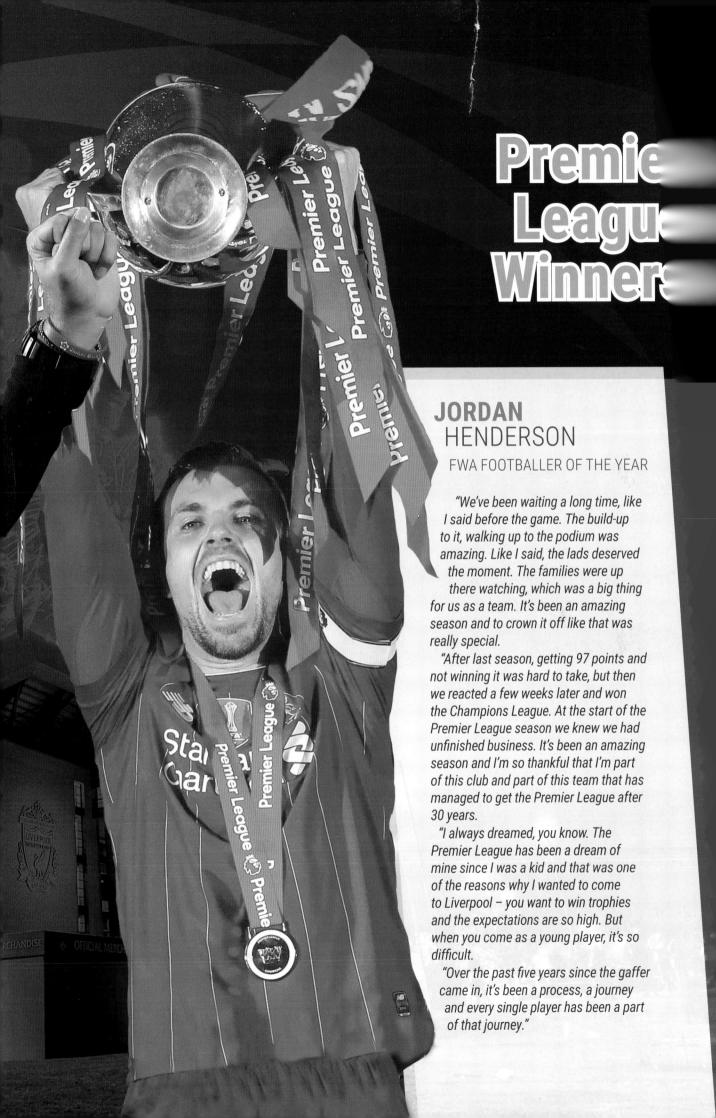

JORDAN
HENDERSON
FWA FOOTBALLER OF THE YEAR

"We've been waiting a long time, like I said before the game. The build-up to it, walking up to the podium was amazing. Like I said, the lads deserved the moment. The families were up there watching, which was a big thing for us as a team. It's been an amazing season and to crown it off like that was really special.

"After last season, getting 97 points and not winning it was hard to take, but then we reacted a few weeks later and won the Champions League. At the start of the Premier League season we knew we had unfinished business. It's been an amazing season and I'm so thankful that I'm part of this club and part of this team that has managed to get the Premier League after 30 years.

"I always dreamed, you know. The Premier League has been a dream of mine since I was a kid and that was one of the reasons why I wanted to come to Liverpool – you want to win trophies and the expectations are so high. But when you come as a young player, it's so difficult.

"Over the past five years since the gaffer came in, it's been a process, a journey and every single player has been a part of that journey."

VIRGIL
VAN DIJK

"We finally get our hands on the Premier League trophy and it's a dream come true for all of us. It has been quite a long wait for all the Liverpool fans around the world and for us obviously. It's just a great feeling, a fantastic feeling to say that I'm a Premier League champion and the rest of the boys as well.

"It's very difficult to stay consistent, as we were this year. When we played the last game of last season against Wolves, Brighton were losing and in the end City won it there. Obviously we were disappointed, but it was like, 'we're going to get it next year'. That's the feeling that we all had.

"The focus that the manager, especially, has brought in is that each game that's ahead of you, that's the most important thing. We're not going to focus on what's two weeks in advance, we focus on the game ahead of us. If it's Wednesday or Saturday, we don't think further. That mentality helped us a lot.

"We always find a way to win, we've been doing it all season. We had big results – Aston Villa away and Wolves away – those kind of moments where we just dig deep, find a way and got the result that we needed.

"It's the mentality of the group of players that we have, the hard work that we put in during training every day and this group of players is very special. We're out there on the pitch, everyone gets along with each other, on the pitch everyone is there to help each other, everyone wants to fight for each other. That's the least that the Liverpool fans want to see from us and that's what we all want from ourselves, too."

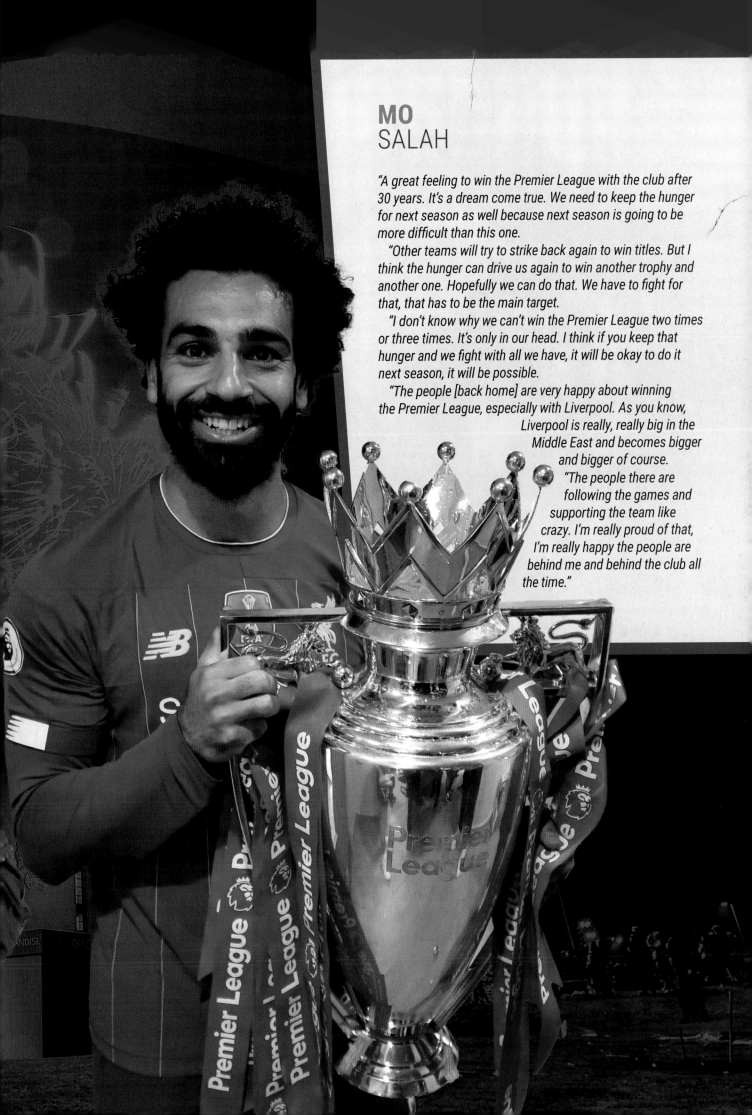

MO
SALAH

"A great feeling to win the Premier League with the club after 30 years. It's a dream come true. We need to keep the hunger for next season as well because next season is going to be more difficult than this one.

"Other teams will try to strike back again to win titles. But I think the hunger can drive us again to win another trophy and another one. Hopefully we can do that. We have to fight for that, that has to be the main target.

"I don't know why we can't win the Premier League two times or three times. It's only in our head. I think if you keep that hunger and we fight with all we have, it will be okay to do it next season, it will be possible.

"The people [back home] are very happy about winning the Premier League, especially with Liverpool. As you know, Liverpool is really, really big in the Middle East and becomes bigger and bigger of course.

"The people there are following the games and supporting the team like crazy. I'm really proud of that, I'm really happy the people are behind me and behind the club all the time."

ALEX
OXLADE-CHAMBERLAIN

"You can't take moments and nights like this for granted. You can't take playing for an amazing football club like this with fans that care so much, you can't take that for granted. So, as a player you need to seize those sorts of moments.

"We are here for a short time. We have our little spells hopefully making history at this football club, we've got to do our bit to inspire the next generation like Steven Gerrard inspired me.

"At the minute we are going that way to doing that, but we need to go on now and have a strong streak for a few years. Once all said and done, that will be our story told and this football club will go on and hopefully people can follow us too. But we've got more work to do here and it's an amazing start to a journey.

"We've done really well in the last three years since I've been here and we need to just keep building on it, but it's a good time to be a Liverpool player and to be involved in this amazing football club.

"I'm really looking forward to what comes next, but we need to stay hungry and stay focused."

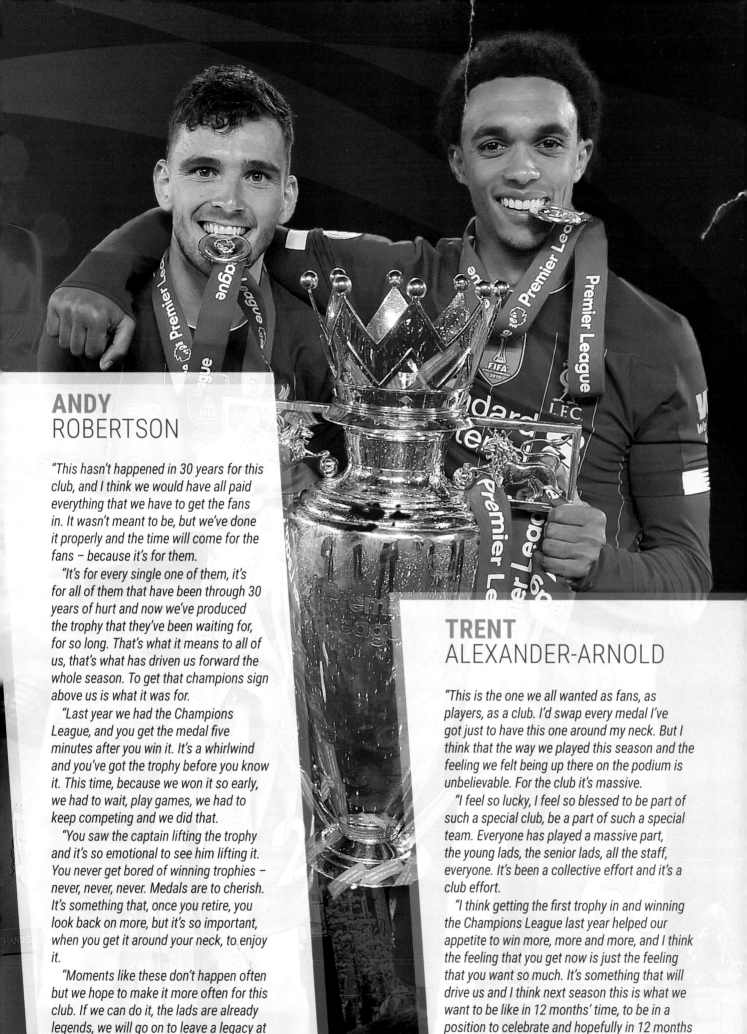

ANDY
ROBERTSON

"This hasn't happened in 30 years for this club, and I think we would have all paid everything that we have to get the fans in. It wasn't meant to be, but we've done it properly and the time will come for the fans – because it's for them.

"It's for every single one of them, it's for all of them that have been through 30 years of hurt and now we've produced the trophy that they've been waiting for, for so long. That's what it means to all of us, that's what has driven us forward the whole season. To get that champions sign above us is what it was for.

"Last year we had the Champions League, and you get the medal five minutes after you win it. It's a whirlwind and you've got the trophy before you know it. This time, because we won it so early, we had to wait, play games, we had to keep competing and we did that.

"You saw the captain lifting the trophy and it's so emotional to see him lifting it. You never get bored of winning trophies – never, never, never. Medals are to cherish. It's something that, once you retire, you look back on more, but it's so important, when you get it around your neck, to enjoy it.

"Moments like these don't happen often but we hope to make it more often for this club. If we can do it, the lads are already legends, we will go on to leave a legacy at this club and that's what we want to do."

TRENT
ALEXANDER-ARNOLD

"This is the one we all wanted as fans, as players, as a club. I'd swap every medal I've got just to have this one around my neck. But I think that the way we played this season and the feeling we felt being up there on the podium is unbelievable. For the club it's massive.

"I feel so lucky, I feel so blessed to be part of such a special club, be a part of such a special team. Everyone has played a massive part, the young lads, the senior lads, all the staff, everyone. It's been a collective effort and it's a club effort.

"I think getting the first trophy in and winning the Champions League last year helped our appetite to win more, more and more, and I think the feeling that you get now is just the feeling that you want so much. It's something that will drive us and I think next season this is what we want to be like in 12 months' time, to be in a position to celebrate and hopefully in 12 months we'll be able to celebrate with the fans."

THE **REDS** ACHIEVED ALL KINDS OF RECORDS IN 2019/20. HERE ARE **19** OF THE BEST...

V NORWICH CITY AT ANFIELD

Liverpool extended their run of scoring at least four goals in a single league game every season since 1920/21, the longest run in England.

V SOUTHAMPTON AT ST MARY'S

Jürgen Klopp became the quickest Reds' manager to reach 300 points (in the three points for a win system) in his 146th game.

V BURNLEY AT TURF MOOR

The first Brazilian to score a 50 goals in English football's top-flight? Roberto Firmino.

V NEWCASTLE UNITED AT ANFIELD

Sadio Mane went half-a-century of games unbeaten at one stadium for the same club, a Premier League first.

V CHELSEA AT STAMFORD BRIDGE

Liverpool won their opening six matches of a top division season for a second consecutive seasons, which had never happened before.

V EVERTON AT ANFIELD

Not since 1982 had LFC scored five goals against Everton and it was the first time they'd hit the Blues for five at Anfield since 1965.

V WATFORD AT ANFIELD

Sunderland in 1891/92 were the last team to win 16 consecutive top-flight games while scoring at least twice. Liverpool matched that with a 2-0 win against the Hornets.

V LEICESTER CITY AT KING POWER STADIUM

Roberto Firmino's second goal in a 4-0 win was the 500th scored by the Reds under Jürgen Klopp.

The Champions W

League Titles

European Cup/ UEFA Champions League

FA Cups

UEFA Cups

League Cups

19

6

7

3

8

V WOLVERHAMPTON WANDERERS AT ANFIELD

The Reds made it 50 home top-flight league games unbeaten, only the third team to ever achieve that.

V SHEFFIELD UNITED AT ANFIELD

Another win made it a calendar year since Liverpool had lost a Premier League game.

V TOTTENHAM HOTSPUR AT TOTTENHAM HOTSPUR STADIUM

A 1-0 win made it 61 points from 21 games, a points tally never before collected in any of the big five European leagues.

V MANCHESTER UNITED AT ANFIELD

Virgil van Dijk's goal meant Liverpool had scored in each of their opening 22 league games, a new first for the club.

V WEST HAM UNITED AT LONDON STADIUM

Preston North End, in 1888/89, beat the other 11 teams in English football's top-flight by 9th February. Liverpool beat the other 19 teams in the top division by 29th January with this win.

V SOUTHAMPTON AT ANFIELD

The Reds made it 43 top-division league games undefeated, the second longest run without losing.

V BOURNEMOUTH AT ANFIELD

Liverpool FC won an English record 22nd consecutive top-flight league game at home, beating the record of 21 set by Bill Shankly's Liverpool FC in 1972.

V ASTON VILLA AT ANFIELD

The Redmen recorded a 24th consecutive home league victory at Anfield, extending their top-flight record.

V BRIGHTON & HOVE ALBION AT AMEX STADIUM

Jürgen Klopp's champions won their 30th game of the season, becoming only the seventh side to do so in the highest tier of English football.

V CHELSEA AT ANFIELD

Another Anfield season concluded without a defeat, making it three years in row unbeaten at home, a new club record.

V NEWCASTLE UNITED AT ST JAMES' PARK

Liverpool's 3-1 victory made it a club record 14 away top-flight wins and the took the Reds to a club record 99 points.

UEFA Super Cups

FIFA Club World Cup

4

1

FINAL PREMIER LEAGUE TABLE **2019/20**

		P	W	D	L	GF	GA	GD	PTS
C	Liverpool	38	32	3	3	85	33	52	99
2	Manchester City	38	26	3	9	102	35	67	81
3	Manchester United	38	18	12	8	66	36	30	66
4	Chelsea	38	20	6	12	69	54	15	66
5	Leicester City	38	18	8	12	67	41	26	62
6	Tottenham Hotspur	38	16	11	11	61	47	14	59
7	Wolverhampton Wanderers	38	15	14	9	51	40	11	59
8	Arsenal	38	14	14	10	56	48	8	56
9	Sheffield United	38	14	12	12	39	39	0	54
10	Burnley	38	15	9	14	43	50	-7	54
11	Southampton	38	15	7	16	51	60	-9	52
12	Everton	38	13	10	15	44	56	-12	49
13	Newcastle United	38	11	11	16	38	58	-20	44
14	Crystal Palace	38	11	10	17	31	50	-19	43
15	Brighton and Hove Albion	38	9	14	15	39	54	-15	41
16	West Ham United	38	10	9	19	49	62	-13	39
17	Aston Villa	38	9	8	21	41	67	-26	35
18	Bournemouth	38	9	7	22	40	65	-25	34
19	Watford	38	8	10	20	36	64	-28	34
20	Norwich City	38	5	6	27	26	75	-49	21